T0318825

Spirits in the Consulting Room

Rutgers Global Health

Series Editor: Javier I. Escobar

Spirits in the Consulting Room

Eight Tales of Healing

SERGE BOUZNAH AND
CATHERINE LEWERTOWSKI

Translated by Carmella Abramowitz Moreau
Foreword by Jaswant Guzder

Rutgers University Press

New Brunswick, Camden, and Newark, New Jersey, and London

Library of Congress Cataloging-in-Publication Data
Names: Bouznah, Serge, author. | Lewertowski, Catherine, author. |
Abramowitz-Moreau, Carmella, translator. | Guzder, Jaswant, writer of foreword.
Title: Spirits in the consulting room : eight tales of healing / Serge Bouznah
and Catherine Lewertowski ; translated by Carmella Abramowitz Moreau ;
foreword by Jaswant Guzder.
Other titles: Quand les esprits viennent aux médecins. English Description:
New Brunswick, New Jersey : Rutgers University Press, [2023] | Series: Rutgers
global health | Translation of: Quand les esprits viennent aux médecins :
7 récits pour soigner. | Includes bibliographical references and index.
Identifiers: LCCN 2022009344 | ISBN 9781978829879 (hardback) |
ISBN 9781978829862 (paperback) | ISBN 9781978829886 (epub) |
ISBN 9781978829893 (pdf)
Subjects: LCSH: Transcultural medical care—France—Case studies. |
Immigrants—Medical care—France—Case studies. | Physician and patient—
France—Case studies. | BISAC: SOCIAL SCIENCE / Disease & Health Issues |
SOCIAL SCIENCE / Anthropology / Cultural & Social
Classification: LCC RA418.5.T73 B6813 2023 | DDC 362.1086/912044—dc23/
eng/20220628
LC record available at https://lccn.loc.gov/2022009344

A British Cataloging-in-Publication record for this book is available
from the British Library.

References to internet websites (URLs) were accurate at the time of writing.
Neither the author nor Rutgers University Press is responsible for URLs that may
have expired or changed since the manuscript was prepared.

♾ The paper used in this publication meets the requirements of the
American National Standard for Information Sciences—Permanence of
Paper for Printed Library Materials, ANSI Z39.48-1992.

www.rutgersuniversitypress.org

Manufactured in the United States of America

With this book, we hope to share with healthcare professionals and patients our pioneering experience in mediation in a hospital setting. To maintain confidentiality, no family names have been mentioned. First names, professions, places, and dates have been changed.

In memory of Oliver Sacks

Contents

Series Foreword

JAVIER I. ESCOBAR

Spirits in the Consulting Room is the third in the Rutgers Global Health book series. The book has been already published in France (Éditions in Press, Paris) and Italy (Editione Colibri, Milan). This English-language version was thoroughly revised to include a detailed prologue that incorporates key references relevant to North America, notably those of Arthur Kleinman and Byron Good.

The first author, Dr. Serge Bouznah, is a Tunisian-born medical doctor practicing in Paris, France. He is the initiator of "transcultural mediation"—a strategy more than two decades old that continues to be actively used in cross-cultural practice.

In the book, the transcultural mediations, or consultations, are nicely illustrated using detailed, colorful, clinical vignettes, in addition to follow-up observations, discussion of key issues, and descriptions of clinical outcomes. These vignettes incorporate a unique format and a team approach based on Devereux's ethnopsychiatric perspective and Nathan's psychotherapeutic techniques. Interestingly, George Devereux, a Hungarian-French researcher, the founder of ethnopsychiatry, spent time in the United States, studying anthropology at the University of California, Berkeley, and worked at the legendary Menninger Clinic in Topeka, Kansas. During his time in the United States, he did extensive research on Native Americans, returning to France for the last portion of his career. After his death, he was buried in an Indian reservation in Colorado.

The first seven clinical "tales" focus on African immigrants to France, coming from several countries, each with specific cultural repertoires that impact the clinical presentations of the various cases. Countries represented in these vignettes are the Democratic Republic of the Congo in Central Africa (two cases), Guinea, Mali, and Senegal, located in Western Africa (one case each), as well Tunisia, located in Northern Africa, and Madagascar, an island country considered as part of Southern Africa (also, one case each).

The eighth and final clinical "tale" relates to a French-born individual and highlights the influence on the clinical presentation of cultural, religious, and national elements. It is an example of how "culture" continues to permeate throughout different generations.

The book is unique, and to my knowledge, no book published in North America offers such a unique content and perspectives or provides such clinical richness and descriptive detail. The book is a rich source of cultural nuances, presented in a detailed, sequential fashion and written with gusto, utilizing a unique literary style. The crux of the book, quoting the authors, is that "the narrative of the patient is always singular, always exceptional."

These clinical tales are reminiscent of those famous neurological tales told by the late neuroscientist, Oliver Sacks. So, it is not surprising, given this similarity, that the book is dedicated to this illustrious English scholar, who crafted colorful neurological tales such as *The Man Who Mistook His Wife for a Hat*.

To the North American reader, the book highlights a unique perspective that may be quite valuable in clinical settings, as highlighted by Kirmayer et al. (2003).

Spirits in the Consulting Room also provides rich descriptions of the worries and fears of African immigrants. The focus on the African diaspora and the perpetuation of cultural traits through various generations will make this a very valuable book for those interested in the cultural aspects of medical practice.

Foreword

JASWANT GUZDER

There are a few times in life when you leap up and the past that
you'd been standing on falls away behind you, and the future you
mean to land on is not yet in place, and for a moment you're
suspended knowing nothing and no one, not even yourself.
—Ann Patchett, *The Dutch House*

In this unique contribution to ethnopsychiatry, Dr. Serge Bouznah
and Dr. Catherine Lewertowski share extraordinary stories that
emerge from a process of "transcultural mediation" for patients of
diverse migrant lineages presenting with serious and unresponsive
medical conditions. The therapeutic focus of the doctors encour-
ages explorations of the internalized, relational, and lived cultural experience of their patients, while also exploring and
opening the possibility of healing pathways that include doors
to the possible influences of "invisible stories" and "irreconcilable
worlds" of Otherness, alternate imaginations, ancestors, and spirits. These methodologies of transcultural mediation are presented
in the form of eight exceptional clinical and culturally embedded narratives of a majority of African migrant patients and their
families who had been referred to cultural specialists because
they presented perplexing symptoms or had otherwise arrived at
an impasse in treatment.

Each vignette accompanies the subjects into imaginary worlds where the clinicians become acquainted with each patient's wider circles of internal and familial actors, both living and deceased, originating in worlds far away from France. In fact, this book could be read twice, initially as a travelogue, as we accompany two wise clinicians and their patients, welcoming spirits into the consulting room to take part in healing trajectories and travel between worlds, formulating prescriptions for unresolved conflicts or encouraging personal encounters that generate possible solutions. The second level of this book is the clinical mediation approaches suggested, as the therapists encourage the patients to access and explore their personal or alternate frameworks, beliefs, possibilities, and solutions that emerge as possibilities, coming out of the apparent disclosures from previously invisible worlds. These particular chosen narratives allow the reader to witness a range of solutions and outcomes that spring from entry into culturally embedded ways of knowing, relational networks of families, and the territories inhabited by ghosts, ancestors, rituals, and beliefs. As each story transverses the boundaries of death and life, the therapist attunes to the patient's unspoken life experience intertwined with their belief systems, intimacy, and structural realities. At the outset of the text, the authors offer an appropriate dictum for the reader to prepare for this journey, with Aimé Césaire's quotation, "Culture is everything that man has invented to make life more livable and death easier to confront."

Implicitly, the authors challenge healthcare providers to recognize the complex implications of deeply embedded personal realities that mirror the diversity of generational immigrants' lived experiences as a valuable potential aspect in the healing context. While there is movement toward cultural mediation and consultation in training, immigration narratives tend to give positive valence to rapid acculturation, mirrored in the "melting pot" theory, colonial resonances, or reflected by the French and Quebecois inscription of secularism (concept of *la laïcité*) as a healthy foundation of a homogenous society. Indeed, there are very few clinical texts that address the important contributions of spiritual or nether worlds. Carlos Sluzki's book *The Presence of the Absent:*

Therapy with Families and Their Ghosts is one of the few that previously explored therapy stories intertwined with the psychic content of spirits or beliefs. Alternative life cycles or the developmental aims of other cultural worlds are also rarely discussed; nor is it common to hear discussions of clinical or systemic possibilities that integrate hauntology or ethnography of indigenous or global diversity in training centers. In this context, Bouznah and Lewertowski have chosen to present each patient narrative as a basic teaching paradigm, as suggested by the premise of a Yiddish proverb "Do not ask the doctor, ask the patient."

"Being with" spirits calls forth "a politics of memory, of inheritance and of generations," to quote Derrida (1994), who named hauntology as a powerful ontology. He reminded us that we may repress the ghosts of histories yet remain haunted as living societies by "forgotten" generational patterns that fundamentally organize relational and affective life, not only impacting individual health and processes of grief, but also problem solving within systems, families, lineage, or collectives with social and political implications. Freud's commentaries on the "return of the repressed" is about not only our individual psyche but also our collective emotional worlds, where generations and ghosts have continued within us as imprinted ways of knowing, patterns, paradigms, and ritualized pathways. The valuable lesson of *Spirits in the Consulting Room* is to reconsider these elements as part of what Bion termed "the felt unthought," and in many cultural contexts as historically essential to imaginative maps for healing and shaping current relational realities.

Indeed, the stories of the spirit world repeatedly underline the error of supposing that memory traces or histories disappear rather than "haunt" us. Spirits, as these many stories tell us, can survive in various forms that can be revived in healing circles, and under certain conditions can be invited to emerge from their hiding places to speak to how they may be helping or hindering well-being.

Professor Jaswant Guzder
McGill University, Psychiatry
Instagram @duartroad

Spirits in the Consulting Room

Prologue:
"When I was two years old, I killed my grandmother"

We could see in any revolt and in any ardour a
personal pain transfigured; what of it?
—Éric Vuillard, *The War of the Poor*

In the years following the independence of Tunisia in 1956, the Jewish community began leaving the country. During the Bizerte Crisis,[1] a conflict between France and Tunisia in summer 1961, anti-Jewish demonstrations triggered new waves of departures. A community that had been settled there for more than 2,000 years, numbering more than 100,000 people, was suddenly reduced to some 3,000 souls living mainly in Djerba and the metropolis of Tunis.

My family was caught up in this maelstrom of history. I was only a child, and no one asked what I thought.

I arrived in France in September 1961; I was six years old. The day we left Tunisia, as we stood on the deck of the ship leaving the port of Tunis, my mother told me our departure was final and my father would join us later. Of the crossing, my only recollection is of a raging sea and the foul odors from the toilets—few and far between—in the hold.

Until then, my childhood in Tunis had been filled with light, noises, and smells that I miss to this very day.

Was this abrupt departure absolutely necessary? What would my life have been without this rupture? What would my story have been?

With the passing of time, I realize how profoundly these early years affected me and, very likely, how they nudged me toward a career in medicine and the field of mediation.

Un Été à la Goulette (A Summer in La Goulette) is not only the title of a film but also a time machine that brings back echoes of the past, filled with images snatched from oblivion, as fragile as fireflies that light up my memory.

Memories. I am lost, wandering on the beach under a blazing sun, until Mabrouk, our family handyman, arrives with a cheerful smile, relieved to find me after hours of searching. Between the moment when I fall asleep on the beach and when I am woken to see Mabrouk, all that remains is a black hole, probably due to that scorching sun.

And then the stories filled with extraordinary people—stories that Pipo, my grandfather, told me. Every evening, in a new story, Zorro, the masked avenger astride Tornado, his indomitable mustang, once again escaped the traps set by El Lobo, the Mexican bandit. How could I have guessed that Pipo was transmitting his gift of storytelling to me?

I am four years old, attending the nursery school run by the Catholic nuns in the Halfouine neighborhood, near my house on Rue Bab Souika. There, I learn to read. More importantly, I first see gangster movies starring Eddie Constantine. When school is out, sometimes my father comes to fetch me, bringing pistachios or a candy apple whose taste I can still savor.

I am playing marbles on Place des Potiers near my home. I cross the street, and a taxi runs into me accidentally. I emerge relatively unscathed, but the angry crowd turns on the reckless driver and then carries me to the home of my paternal grandfather, Houatou. The scene ends with the burning in my throat as I swallow the local distilled fig brandy, *boukha*, that my aunts give me to perk me up.

And then more images of La Goulette in our summer house. I'm jumping onto my grandmother's bed, and she bursts out laughing. But the memory of that moment of joy is shattered by my mother's order, "Stop that immediately. You'll kill your grandmother." Prophetic words, indeed, that drew the evil eye.

Some time after that, my grandmother died of heart failure at the Tunis Hospital. I remember my mother collapsing on the staircase to our apartment. I remember her cries, more like interminable screams that nothing or no one could stop, least of all myself, a small, terrified child. I remember neither my sadness nor my tears, but rather the shock that stunned me, turning me into a cold, mute figurine.

Nearly thirty years later, when I was beginning my psychoanalysis, I plucked up the courage to ask my mother about the cause of the vague feeling I had sensed in her since then, of some sort of anger toward me, her child. And I can't begin to describe the intense relief that overwhelmed me when she said, with a sincerity I can only admire, that in the days that followed her mother's death, she resented me bitterly, for I showed no feelings. Thirty years later, we were finally able to cry together and then, a few years after, to go to my grandmother's tomb in the Borgel Cemetery in Tunis.

I like to think that making amends for the death of a grandmother and appeasing the pain of a mother is driving force enough for an entire lifetime. And so, the path to medicine, and then to mediation, was opened.

Forty Years On

Catherine Lewertowski: Serge, we should begin by explaining to our readers why we have written this book—why we want to give a voice to those whom we hear so little yet who have so much to teach us.

Serge Bouznah: I think we should start with ourselves, with our own experience, and what has gone into making us doctors. We should talk about the enriching quality of our training, as well as our rebellions against the hospital, which is a world apart. On entering it, a human being becomes a body on public view, a body without a history or a culture.

Catherine L.: That's no surprise when you start learning medicine by working on a cadaver. When I was a young medical student, the first shock for me was dissecting a body in the silence of an anatomical pathology lab. We underwent our initiation on a dead body. Only after that did we have to confront words in the hospital. But what words! Words that are murmured between specialists, with no one else in earshot, in the hallways, in the staff rooms, or words pronounced—sometimes all too bluntly—to a vulnerable patient. At the time, I saw the hospital as a temple of the words of the experts; they were words without feeling. But that is also how you "make" a doctor of yourself: keeping your distress pent up to become a technician who works with the body. Yet, emotion penetrated each and every one among us, and no matter how overwhelmed we were, there was no question of expressing any sort of discomfort. I was never able to reconcile myself to this strategy of camouflage.

Serge B.: My turning point came when my paternal uncle fell ill. He was barely forty years old when he was diagnosed with advanced cancer. I was a third-year medical student. He was rushed to the Hôtel Dieu hospital in central Paris, where his condition worsened rapidly. According to his consulting physicians, there was no hope for him. As a last resort, our family consulted a rav^2 of the Sephardi community, who carried out the prescribed ceremony for a patient in mortal danger: he changed my uncle's name.[3] Sadly, this ritual did not change the course of the disease. In desperation, my uncle's wife called on a very controversial specialist in bacteriology, Jean Solomidès. In the 1950s, this researcher claimed to have discovered a treatment that would revolutionize cancer treatment, altering the prognosis dramatically. He had developed synthetic anticancer "physiatrons." My relatives did not hesitate; they were willing to try anything. They asked me to explain the family's wishes to the head of the unit caring for my uncle and, more importantly, to convince him to give my uncle the potion concocted by Dr. Solomidès. I gave him the vial. Up to this very day, I still remember his disdainful smirk. It was like a slap in my face—one that I can still feel. I suspect that he never gave the brew to my uncle. This was just folk medicine for him, and there was no place in the hospital for folk medicine. He was indifferent to the suffering of my family members, their hope for some sort of peace, even psychological appeasement. For him, it was only the scientific perspective that counted.

Catherine L.: And that was perhaps the first time you found yourself caught between two irreconcilable worlds: the world into which you were born and which made you what you are and the world of medicine that was opening its arms to you. I'm not sure that you believed in Solomidès's treatment, but you remained loyal to your family.

Serge B.: You're right, it was a problem of loyalty. You and I are both children of immigrant families, and we have often wondered where we belong. Are we part of our original cultural group, or are we part of the society that took in our families? Does choosing one mean betraying the other? We have asked ourselves the question so often, without ever really deciding, that we have become, I believe, go-betweens, mediating between two worlds and different systems of thinking. While my uncle was dying, I was not ready to construct such bridges. But for the first time, I felt that it was vitally important.

Catherine L.: We should make it clear that we are by no means denigrating medicine and all the good it does. In this book, we will relate our encounters with people afflicted with serious medical conditions, and recount how we learn about their stories. We will show that for each medical narrative, there is almost always another narrative to echo it, often unknown to the hospital staff—one that is told within the family circle. These other narratives are no less logical and no less coherent. They are there, lurking, ready to surge out if only we are ready to listen. They give meaning to what is happening and help patients to resist and to act. And sometimes, even, they can help cure them. But the potency of these narratives is completely foreign to Western medical logic. Aimé Césaire once said, "Culture is everything that man has invented to make life more livable and death easier to confront"[4] (my translation).

I suggest we make his phrase the dictum of our book.

Introduction

I realize that the failure of twenty-four excellent physicians can only mean
we have reached the limits of contemporary medical knowledge
—Irvin David Yalom, *When Nietzsche Wept*

Freg nisht dem royfe, freg dem choyle.
[Do not ask the doctor, ask the patient.]
—Yiddish Proverb

Our work involves negotiating transactions. Over the years, we
have become bridge builders between our fellow physicians and
their patients, mediating between the techniques of the former and
the unseen knowledge of the latter.

A World in Transformation

The death of a young boy in the pediatric unit of a large Paris
hospital. The child came from another place—a place called Tizi
Ouzou in Algeria. He was flown to Paris on his own and then
entrusted into the care of a French host family before being moved
to the hospital. He liked to share stories with his nursing auxiliary.
She too was Kabyle, and so they spoke the same language. He was
due to undergo a bone marrow transplantation in an attempt to
save him from the disease that had already taken his two brothers.
That morning, when the physician returned to the ward, he found
the nursing auxiliary leaning over the body of the child. She was

7

washing him, and as she worked, she murmured words in her native language. Later, the doctor learned that the woman had practiced the sacred rites due to the dead on the child, just as she would have done for a member of her family.

Enter the waiting room of any hospital in a large metropolis and you will immediately be struck by the diverse cultural origins of the patients. Hospitals, a microcosm of the world, have long been multicultural. Within the hospital, patients of diverse identities and many nationalities speaking countless languages are treated side by side. Each one has their particular vision of illness, suffering, and death. But does this cultural intermingling change anything in the medical care given to the suffering patients?

An encounter with our Western medical system does not seem to pose any particular problem to the majority of the patients. Yet, during discussions with physicians on changing trends, most mention increasingly frequent cases of misunderstanding and mutual incomprehension. What are the reasons that make the healthcare provider–migrant patient relationship more difficult? Linguistic difficulties are regularly mentioned (Pergert et al., 2007; Hsieh, 2016), but everyone will admit that, fundamentally, this is not sufficient an explanation. Does this signify that the cultural difference between healthcare providers and migrant patients is the cause? In France, raising the subject is tantamount to treading on a minefield. The French Revolution established the principle of equality between all individuals, whatever their community or class, and inscribed secularism (*la laïcité*) as a founding principle of the new state. This means that recognizing and accepting plurality is a perilous exercise. The expression of plural identities and modes of thinking is, today, still too often interpreted as proof of resistance to integration, an affront to the host society. Given no other alternative, it is far easier for healthcare providers to smooth over any differences behind a facade of universality, however far removed it is from the reality the families experience daily.

In view of these observations, we must find a way to work with the diversity we encounter. We do not seek to reduce individuals to their culture, nor to reduce the problems encountered with migrant patients to the cultural distance that supposedly separates us (Verrept, 2008). This culturalist position is, of course, simplistic; it is not particularly helpful in thinking through the complexity of human relationships. With more than twenty years of clinical experience, we hope to show that in situations where Western medicine has reached an impasse, taking into account cultural issues—considering them not as an obstacle but as a remarkably effective catalyst—enriches the medical interpretation. Furthermore, it enables a meeting of minds between patient and physician. To take the matter even further, the process of introducing cultural issues into a medical care relationship goes beyond merely probing the patient's particular vision of their illness so that they will accept the medical solutions proposed. It also involves a symmetrical questioning of the world of the physicians, their theory, and the logic of their procedures to explain them to the families. This exercise is by no means self-evident. To proceed honestly, we must free ourselves from a binary mode of thinking that all too often opposes the word of the patient to the incontestable truth of medical and scientific discourse. It must be acknowledged that where the word of experts is pitted against the word of the layperson, the expert always prevails. Bearing this in mind is a first step in clarifying the specificity of the medical encounter with migrants. The distance that may separate our universes of thought, our representations of the world, and, more specifically, the ways in which we explain misfortune and illness compels us to renounce our inertia, critique our professional practices, and even invent new procedures so that we can give these patients supportive care. If we embrace this new position and the magnifying glass that migrant patients hold up to us, so to speak, they become our guides, enabling us to explore the complexity of the healthcare provider–patient relationship with even greater lucidity.

Let Us Take a Closer Look

There are two narratives around the semantic pair *disease/illness*; most often, their paths do not intersect. The narrative of disease concerns the physician, who is the professional, a technician specialized in the human body. It is constructed based on the symptoms of the patient; its objective is above all to provide a diagnosis and therapy. The physician works from proofs that underlie scientific truth. The second narrative, the illness, is that of the patient. It concerns existential questions—Why me? Why now?—and helps give meaning to a potentially fatal intrusion into their life. This quest for meaning when dealing with grave illness is universal. It goes beyond the search for the causes on which the physician's attention focuses. At once individual and collective, it weaves a narrative thread in the life experience of each of us, taking as its source the collective interpretations of illness and misfortune specific to each community.

These two narratives are different by nature; generally, each community is unaware of that of the other. The discourse of medicine pronounces the official viewpoint on disease and claims the monopoly on its definition. For Western medicine, disease is one and the same; it is universal. Tubercular meningitis is identical in Bamako and in Los Angeles. However, the narrative of the patient is always singular, always exceptional. Patients do not seek to establish the truth but rather to construct a meaning. The appearance of an illness may be interpreted as a message to the patient and perhaps also to the group. This second narrative is not necessarily disconnected from medical thought. It has a complex relationship with the medical discourse that may range from total adhesion to open competition (Taïeb et al., 2005). In our clinical conversations, we see that a patient may acknowledge that their disease is due to the HIV[1] retrovirus or tubercle bacillus, all the while explaining that it is the secret weapon in an act of sorcery against them. In previous research on children infected with HIV and their families (Nathan and Lewertowski, 1998), we demonstrated that the interpretation of patients with lay knowledge does not preclude a fine understanding of medical discourse. Furthermore, their interpretations are not necessarily an obstacle to establishing a therapeutic alliance.

The construction of an individual narrative in sessions of mediation is often based on what anthropologists call a typical plot (Good, 1994) or laypeople's etiological theories[2] (Taïeb et al., 2005). These are culturally coded statements concerning the causes and meaning of the illness, available to the subject by virtue of their belonging to a group. Transmitted in various forms, they are sufficiently general and implicit to be relevant to all individuals in the same cultural group. These typical plots do not de facto impose themselves, nor are they unequivocal; furthermore, they are dynamic, may be discussed, and can evolve. An individual can take full or partial ownership of such coded statements, depending on the psychic costs involved, and prior to constructing an individual meaning. Patients use their culture as a type of lexicon that enables them to find typical plots to produce an individual narrative.

In our hospital units, where the theories of disease put forward by the medical profession prevail, other explanatory models (those of the patients and their families) often resonate, sometimes below the surface. Using these models enables patients to organize their own therapeutic networks in parallel to the hospital treatment they receive. Contrary to preconceived ideas, these practices, often collective, are not the vestiges of archaic beliefs. They are built up within complex systems of thought specific to a group, and dovetail with cultural schemes. They sometimes go far back in history, providing interpretive grids for reading and understanding the world. Naturally, such interpretations might well shock those schooled in the Cartesian tradition who have long freed themselves of their ties with their dead and their patron saints,[3] or even those doctors who accuse parallel therapeutic circuits of exploiting the gullibility of the vulnerable. This is why patients only reveal their recourse to non-biomedical care in exceptional circumstances—they are too worried that it might be immediately dismissed. Yet, the steps they take, in whatever form, are neither part of folklore nor backward beliefs. They are *the* reality of the families we deal with.[4]

In the majority of cases, healthcare providers are totally igno-rant of the world of their patients. And in fact, knowledge of their world is not necessarily useful to doctors . . . except for the patients with whom they have reached an impasse. If we go back to the fourth century B.C., Hippocrates helps us to understand the reasons for this apparent disinterest. The first to attempt to ratio-nalize the link between symptoms and care, he unshackled himself from popular beliefs as well as the influence of the gods. Hip-pocrates stated that if the patient did not collaborate, any therapeu-tic relationship would be incomplete. But in his model, disease is a mystery to which only the doctor holds the key (Grenier in Lecourt, 2004, 308–310). The patient, docile and submissive, must submit to the expert's prescriptions. This trend accelerated over the centuries until it reached extremes. In demanding that disease be objectiv-ized, modern medicine has progressively put aside the patient as a subject from its field of investigation (Canguilhem, 2013). The body of the patient provides access to knowledge of the disease, but the patient's words and subjectivity constitute so many obstacles to the truth of the symptoms (Baszanger, 1995).

Today, thanks to medical progress, increasing numbers of patients live with disease as a constant companion. Anyone with a disease that has become chronic acquires expertise that affects the healthcare provider–patient relationship and forces the two interlocutors into a coexistence previously considered to be an unholy alliance. Doctors have achieved amazing victories. Now, they have to take up a new challenge that involves sharing respon-sibilities and setting up alliances with people who are suffering.

Our path was shown to us principally by patients—migrants for the most part—affected by grave, chronic diseases that could not be categorized by medical diagnoses. Despite complex treatment and specialized, sometimes very invasive exams, physicians could neither understand nor relieve their ills. Their interpretive grid proved to be inadequate in decrypting the symptoms. We could not remain impassive in the face of their suffering. It was impos-sible not to fulfil our duty to understand and allay their distress.

These "atypical" patients helped us to identify the shortcomings and gaps in our system; they indicated where we should explore uncharted routes and widen our expertise to better our art of healing. By listening to them, we acquired knowledge we could not have dreamed of. Today, this knowledge enables us to offer teams of healthcare providers in a therapeutic dead end an original clinical process: transcultural mediation.

Multiple Influences

Medical anthropology, ethnopsychiatry, and narrative-based medicine are the theoretical pillars on which we have constructed our clinical system. The work of Arthur Kleinman (1981) and Byron Good (1994) introduced us to the views proposed by the American school of medical anthropology. They were a revelation to us—a blast of fresh air gusting into our hitherto-closed medical milieu. In resonance with this trend, the Division of Social and Transcultural Psychiatry of McGill University has brilliantly demonstrated the relevance of medical anthropology to its work with migrants and refugees in mental health services (Kirmayer et al., 2003, 2014).

To accept the idea that medicine does not give us a direct, objective snapshot of the natural biological order but rather is also rooted in our culture meant we could take a decisive step forward. This view was not easy for many of my colleagues to adopt. They were all trained at French universities, where not an iota of medical anthropology was taught. Despite the richness of the French language, there is only a single word, *maladie*, to encompass the various forms of disease, whether objectively diagnosed or subjectively experienced by a patient. Arthur Kleinman and Byron Good distinguish between "disease"—diagnosed by medicine—and "illness"—a disorder that is experienced. This distinction has enabled them to adopt a critical approach to medical knowledge (de Almeida-Filho, 2006).

For these authors, illness as a social fact is a construction that only exists through the interpretation it is given. Western medicine thus does not hold an exclusive definition of the morbid condition; culture is essential in conceptualizing it as a human reality.

If, as Kleinman shows, the patient and the physician are each the custodian of a specific model that constructs the meaning of the disorder for the one and the disease for the other (Kleinman, 1981), some situations of healthcare provider–patient impasse might well be related to the failure to reach a transaction between the two models. How can negotiation be resumed in such a way as to allow patients to take ownership of the medical model, all the while retaining their own explanatory model?

Ethnopsychiatry, and more specifically the complementarist method put forward by Georges Devereux,[5] suggests a way of associating medical theory and lay interpretation. This is a key challenge, for it determines the legitimacy of the players involved. If the definition of the problem at hand remains exclusively biomedical, the physician—the biomedical expert—is the only one who can act. If, on the other hand, we manage—without in any way refuting the medical interpretation—to construct a larger definition of the disorder with the patient and their family, new players can enter the scene.

Devereux laid the theoretical foundations of complementarism in psychotherapy in situations where therapist and patient came from different cultures (Devereux, 1972). His method enabled the psychotherapist to draw on two complementary forms of discourse: one based on psychoanalysis, and the other on anthropology. By shifting psychotherapy to the field of medicine, we have adapted the method to the specificity of our interventions. We must thus hold a double discourse on the illness event, relying on the sources of two disciplines: biomedicine, of course, and anthropology. These discourses intermesh to give rise to a new illness object that both encompasses and goes beyond the medical interpretation. Only with their new knowledge and respective skills can patients and practitioners work together to deal with this new object.

Once Devereux had laid the theoretical foundations of eth-nopsychiatry in 1980, Tobie Nathan pioneered new clinical prac-tices in psychotherapy. Nathan's originality—one might even call it his audacity—consisted in giving valid status to so-called traditional medicines[6] within consultations. There, they were no longer considered as beliefs but rather as veritable logical processes whose efficacy had to be analyzed (Stengers and Nathan, 2012). The technique advocated by Nathan, then developed by Moro (2011), is based on caring for patients in a group setting where their native language becomes an active tool in the therapeutic process. In France, French is often used by the immigrant instrumentally, but the vocabulary of the native language is key in accessing the meaning the subject attributes to events such as illness, suffering, and death.

We have adapted Devereux's theory to our specific mediation sessions in the field of medicine and combined them with the technical framework founded by Nathan to create an entirely new procedure within the hospital.

Transcultural Mediation

We began working with a team of practitioners specialized in pain management at the Centre d'Évaluation et de Traitement de la Douleur (Center for Pain Evaluation and Treatment) at the Fondation Ophtalmologique Adolphe de Rothschild, a public hospital in Paris. Our system was made available to healthcare providers who were confronted with serious difficulties or who had run into a dead end in caring for patients from migrant backgrounds suffering from a chronic painful pathology (Bouznah, Lewertowski, and Margot-Duclot, 2007). The encounter with the pain management team was by no means fortuitous. Chronic pain, an eminently subjective symptom that is difficult to objectivize, means the patient's experience must be taken into account in the treatment plan (Le Breton, 1995). It implies a profound transformation of technical means of care, with longer consultations, multidisciplinary teams, and the determination to use an all-encompassing approach in response to an imperative that is both ethical and technical: place the patient at the center of the treatment plan. Since then, at the request of other units in hospitals in Paris and its surrounding areas, we have widened the scope of our mediation sessions to establish a partnership with Hôpital Necker,[7] another public teaching hospital in Paris, which has enabled transcultural mediation to be incorporated into the hospital's facilities for use by the teams of healthcare providers.

Practitioners opt for a transcultural consultation as a last resort, having exhausted all resources of the biomedical technical facilities, including the opinions of specialized psychiatrists and psychologists. At this stage, doctors are convinced that an exclusively medical response is no longer appropriate. What we strive to facilitate is the unlikely encounter between the world of the practitioner and that of the patient. And that is why the mediation sessions are held in the usual setting where hospital consultations take place, in the presence of the hospital practitioner, who retains full responsibility for the medical care.

The aim of transcultural mediation is to modify a situation and not simply facilitate communication between doctors and patients. Rather, we strive to create a space for transaction to take place as we search for creative solutions. This mediation turns on a key issue: patient and practitioner usually interact within a profoundly unequal relationship. By its very nature, the practitioner–patient relationship is unbalanced. On the one hand, there is the practitioner, an expert in disease, a person usually in good health and perfectly at ease with the codes of society. On the other, there is the patient, presumably ignorant of what is happening to him or her, often isolated, and furthermore, if a migrant, lacking full understanding of the codes and language of the host society. The objective of the transcultural mediation is to address this imbalance.

The group we invite to the consultation disrupts the classic dual relationship of doctor/patient. We bring together the patient and their family, as well as the referring practitioner, the transcultural mediator (who, in our practice, is often a clinical psychologist or an interpreter trained in mediation, familiar with the cultural codes and native language of the patient), and the facilitators of the process. At this new type of staff meeting, held with the patient in attendance, the hospital practitioner plays a central role. He or she takes the time to recount a complex medical history to the family; more importantly, they agree to give serious consideration to the family's interpretations without dismissing them as backward beliefs. The person heading the transcultural mediation session is a physician trained in leading such group encounters. This physician facilitator guarantees the free flow of speech, ensuring that all individuals can express themselves and ask all the questions they might need to. We know only too well that however clearly healthcare providers want to inform patients, patients cannot easily understand the complex data concerning their medical condition. The use of specialized vocabulary, even if geared to nonspecialists, means that the patient cannot access the medical theory underlying the logic of the treatment. This fact is of even greater concern when the disease is serious and chronic and has taken the patient over a long path in search of a cure, shuttled between several specialized units over months and sometimes even years. We take the time we need, and our dual position as third parties and physician facilitator of the consultation allows us to question our hospital colleague about the reasoning that underlies the treatment plan in the presence of the patient and their family. Our role is to oversee all interactions. We must allow all points of view to be expressed and considered equally valid; nothing should be dismissed. By going through the timeline of the facts, we reactivate the medical history and reformulate complex statements; we place whatever has been said that remains misunderstood or obscure in perspective, giving it a new tenor. Once all the questions have been dealt with and the mysteries cleared up, the success of this initial transcultural mediation depends on the abilities of the moderators to explain the complex treatment plan to the patient.

Because we intervene in situations where medical teams are at an impasse as far as treatment plans are concerned, we operate in an area where mainstream medicine agrees to expose the limits of its actions (Bouznah and Larchanché, 2015). By openly accepting these limits in the presence of the patient, the practitioner offers the key to another type of discourse on the disorder. If medicine cannot explain the patient's suffering, and if, in addition, it cannot offer a cure, then healthcare providers are more amenable to taking paths that go far beyond those of mainstream medical action. At this stage of the treatment plan, the powerlessness of medical treatment—however relative—becomes a lever to activate hitherto unknown or underused resources of the patients. And that is why, during the second stage of the transcultural mediation, the patients and their family are given the floor. They reveal their precise, intimate knowledge of their own suffering; their expertise enriches the illness event. With the help of the transcultural mediator, we give them what is often their first opportunity to reveal, in a medical setting, the insightful meaning they attribute to the events that befall them. As active protagonists in the medical relationship, they make a sudden transition from the status of "those who are talked about" to "those with whom we speak" (Baszanger, 1998).

Once both points of view have been expressed, the facilitator puts forward a new narrative in which the medical treatment given acquires meaning in the world of the patient. Previously, the two narratives opposed one another in the shadows, sometimes neutralizing one another.

Now, we bring them together, giving priority to neither, and respecting their differences so that they act in synergy. Thus, the entirety of the resources available are mobilized: those put forward by the practitioner, naturally, as well as the potential of the patient and family. In this new dynamic based on mutual recognition of the legitimacy of everyone's expertise and point of view, healthcare provider, patient, and family at last come together to confront the disorder.

In today's world of healthcare, it is impossible to continue using a new approach without evaluating it. We were happy to respond to this challenge, and research on our method was undertaken. A team from the INSERM, the only French public research organization entirely dedicated to human health, demonstrated the impact of transcultural mediation on the therapeutic alliance. In parallel, another team, specializing in health economics, showed that our treatment has a positive medico-economic impact (Lachal et al., 2019).

In this book, we have elected to tell eight stories about eight encounters that had a particularly profound effect on our practices. They moved us; they exemplify the work we carry out with teams providing healthcare. Most importantly, they enabled patients previously unable to move on to affront their serious disease with new strength.

At the request of doctors who had been caring for the patients for months, sometimes for years, we met with Christelle, Djibril, Alice and Pierre, Moncef, Alhassane, Jacinthe, Amy, and Cyril[8] at a time when, overcome with suffering, despair was draining the life out of them. In the reassuring presence of their practitioners, they agreed to tell us the stories of their illnesses. In giving us a narrative that the medical teams were hitherto unaware of, these patients sometimes feared they would shock us. But we encouraged them to continue. They confided in us, telling us about their doubts and their anger. We were respectful of their courage. But more was required. Working jointly with the patients, we delved beneath the seemingly absurd surface to find rich resources precisely in those places where disease sheds light on the very meaning of life and becomes, paradoxically, a powerful incentive to act.

And now it is time to introduce you to the patients.

1

The Title Deed
of Grandfather Léon

June 2008
Annual pediatric workshops
Main amphitheater, Hôpital Necker Enfants Malades, Paris

Dr. D., who was leading the seminar, clicked on the remote control. "To prepare for this session, I decided to find out how Christelle was doing. We hadn't seen her at the hospital for two years. I called her father, and we had a long chat. He was happy to talk to me—he certainly hadn't forgotten the mediation sessions. He sent me a photo so I could show the whole team how much his daughter had changed."

Immediately a beautiful photo was displayed on the white screen of the amphitheater. Amused, puzzled murmurs rippled through this gathering of white-coated health specialists. The photo showed Nicolas Sarkozy, then president of France, shaking the hand of a glowing, tall, thin girl in the courtyard of a *lycée*, a high school, in the Paris region. For the commemoration of the end of World War II, the president was making an award to a class for their work on the Resistance. The young girl appeared anything but overawed by the solemnity of the occasion. Her mischievous expression contrasted starkly with the gravity of the official delegation. She was barely recognizable to us. But this was indeed Christelle, smiling radiantly at her father behind the camera.

April 2005
Pediatric gastroenterology conference room, Hôpital Necker
Enfants-Malades
In attendance: Christelle, the patient; her parents; three members of
her father's family; three members of her mother's family; four members
of the healthcare team; Geneviève K., the transcultural mediator; Catherine Lewertowski and Serge Bouznah, the two facilitators of the transcultural mediation team

Christelle refused to use the wheelchair, and each step she took
required superhuman effort. Even with the help of her nurse, she
walked with difficulty to the meeting room, clutching on to her
IV pole.[1] Her emaciated hips barely held up her faded jeans. She
was short of breath. A tendril of hair that had slipped from her
braids lay across her face. She looked like a person many times
her age—an elderly woman with no strength left. But Christelle
was only thirteen years old.

To facilitate her treatment, she wore a short hospital gown
that exposed her left shoulder; it was covered with a wide ban-
dage, golden brown with Betadine. That morning, the central
venous catheter[2] for intravenous feeding was not in place. What
did this mean? At the doorway, Christelle stopped for some
time. She lifted her head and somehow found the strength to
flash a smile at the group gathered for her in the pediatric gas-
troenterological conference room; this unit is a leading center in
France for pediatric digestive pathologies. Rarely had there
been so many attendees at a transcultural mediation session.
To seat all the participants, we had to push away the tables and
arrange the chairs in a circle.

At last, Christelle, exhausted and ashen, took a seat in an
armchair someone had rushed out to fetch. As several pillows were
arranged to support her head, her young, malnourished body was
shaken by violent spasms that almost made her vomit. But that
afternoon, Christelle would not vomit. She would spend two hours
listening as her story and that of her family, all from the Democratic Republic of Congo, was recounted.

We had asked her parents to invite all those people who might help us understand what was happening to Christelle. Aunts, uncles, and cousins responded, coming from Paris, Lille, and Strasbourg. And that day, seated around Christelle and her parents were not only the facilitators of the mediation session and the transcultural mediator but also four members of the healthcare providing team: two nurses who worked shifts day and night looking after her, the unit pediatric psychiatrist, and the senior physician who had been treating her since she was hospitalized.

Christelle was losing her strength. No one could understand why. The physicians were faced with a medical situation they could not understand; they could no longer hide their concern.

They feared that Christelle's life was in danger.

Christelle had been hospitalized here for the past four months, since the day when, out of the blue, during a history class at her middle school, she was struck with stabbing abdominal pains. Since then, she had been unable to swallow any food without vomiting uncontrollably. Whenever she tried to eat, her body refused the food; she could hold nothing down. This star student had had to stop attending school. Soon, a central venous catheter had to be put in place to save her from malnutrition. For the past four months, the young girl had undergone increasingly invasive medical exams on a daily basis. Numerous specialists had come to her bedside; not one found a cause for her symptoms. There was no intestinal obstruction and no small intestinal malrotation.[3] They found neither a brain tumor nor cystic fibrosis.[4] All the blood work was practically normal, as were the radiological investigations. Faced with such grave symptoms, an exploratory laparotomy[5] was carried out. The surgeon discovered that her pancreas was as hard as stone, suggesting chronic pancreatitis.[6] But to the specialists, her pancreas was not affected to a degree that would explain the seriousness of her symptoms.

Faced with a situation where there was no obvious diagnosis whatsoever, the medical team suggested that there might be a psychological dimension to the problem. But Christelle said little to the psychiatrist she met with regularly. However, the caregiving team noticed that there was some tension between her parents, who were often at her bedside. But what family conflict could explain clinical features of such gravity? Christelle had already lost more than sixteen pounds,[7] and despite a round-the-clock intravenous painkiller prescribed by her doctor, she could be heard moaning with pain.

When she was initially hospitalized, Christelle was allowed home for the weekend to spend time with her family—she has brothers and sisters. But by our encounter, her condition had deteriorated so significantly that she could no longer leave the hospital. The medical team was powerless to alleviate her suffering. Dr. D., the referring pain physician, suggested they call on a team of transcultural mediators, and the family immediately agreed. The meeting was set up quickly within the hospital department so that everyone—Christelle, her parents, and the team—could participate.

The day prior to the encounter, the physicians had decided to undertake a surgical procedure to remove part of the duodenum and the pancreatic head. In their opinion, there was no doubt that there was an obstruction in the biliary tract, although not a single examination had revealed anything. The aim of the procedure was to remove this obstruction. It was scheduled for four days later.

An Impossible Love Story

There we were, sitting in a circle, the healthcare team on either side of Serge B. and the transcultural mediator, Geneviève K., and the two parents together, flanked by their respective relatives. Christelle, close to Catherine L., was opposite them. Leaning on her right side, she tried to find the most comfortable position. From the outset, the tension was palpable; Christelle's maternal and paternal relatives all appeared to be on their guard. After the customary introductions, the physician, at our request, explained the clinical situation. For more than an hour, he went through the timeline of the medical facts point by point, explaining in the smallest detail the initial symptoms, the hypotheses of diagnosis, and the numerous examinations that had been undertaken, as well as their results. He concluded by saying that the medical team had not, to date, found the cause of Christelle's symptoms. The family listened attentively to the specialist's explanations. Then, each of the other members of the medical team took the floor to testify not only to the young girl's suffering but also to her bravery. Serge B. then asked the family members to speak. All that ensued was a long silence.

Serge B. initiated the dialogue. "In a situation such as this, it's only normal for everyone to wonder what has struck a child so cruelly. If the doctors are powerless to provide an explanation, perhaps it is worth searching for other explanations."

The family remained silent. In an attempt to loosen their tongues, Serge B. called on Geneviève, the transcultural mediator. Quite uncharacteristically for her, she also held back.

Catherine L. addressed Serge B., saying, "If it's so hard to get the words out, perhaps it's because some of those words might be very hurtful to the family members themselves?"

Serge B. resumed, "As you know, all of us—and there are many of us—have gathered today because Christelle's life is in danger. We need to understand what's happening." A man, his face lined with age, finally broke the silence. He was Christelle's paternal uncle, Albert. He turned to Christelle's physicians, saying, "Can I ask you a question? Are you really sure that Western medicine cannot explain what is happening to my niece?"

When they confirmed this, Uncle Albert continued, pointing at Christelle's parents, "All of this has happened because they got married."

Visible discomfort swept over the other family members.

"You know, they are not from the same group, and so there are problems of communication between them," he continued.

Geneviève asked him to explain further, but Albert seemed reluctant to go any further down such a rocky road. It was then that the mediator began speaking in Lingala, the lingua franca of the Democratic Republic of Congo,[8] from whence the two families come. Immediately, a lively discussion arose between the family members. The uncle spoke in a more serious tone; his expression was severe. Albert, like all the other family members present, spoke perfect French, but he now opted to speak in Lingala to explain his thoughts. After a short while, Geneviève interpreted what Albert had said, taking us to the crux of the family belief system.

"This gentleman has explained that Christelle's parents met when they were both studying at university. They got on very well together from the outset; in fact, it was love at first sight. Very soon, they decided to marry, even though both families disapproved strongly of the union."

Serge B. asked why their families were so strongly opposed to the marriage. Geneviève answered, "For a very simple reason: they're not from the same ethnic group. Irène, Christelle's mother, is Bakongo. The Bakongo are an important ethnic group in our country. Romuald, Christelle's father, is Kingwana, an ethnic group that is part of the Swahili group.[9] He comes from the Kindu region in Maniema province. The problem is that the two groups are very different: the majority of the Bakongo are Christian, while the majority of the Swahili are Muslim."

Catherine L. interposed, "So, we could say they are a mixed couple?"

"Exactly. They're both African but from completely different religions and ethnic groups."

Reacting to the intrigued expressions of the healthcare team, Geneviève continued, "You see, the Bakongo are matrilineal, while the Swahili are patrilineal. 'Patrilineal' means that the children are affiliated to the father's clan. And 'matrilineal' means the opposite. The children belong to the mother's line, and the nephews are the heirs of their maternal uncle. All this is completely unlike the way Romuald's family functions."

The psychiatrist now asked Geneviève a question: "But in a matrilineal system, what is the place of the children's father?"

"The biological father plays an educational role and gives the children emotional support. But the children are permanently under the control of the mother's family. Keep in mind that the fathers are responsible for the children of their own sisters, whom they consider their own. Between Christelle's mother's and father's families, everything is different, and not only the rules of filiation, but also those concerning dowries and inheritance. Albert seems to be saying that Christelle's parents did not do what they were supposed to do."

Geneviève could not continue. All of a sudden, her words released a burst of flames that had been smoldering. The room seemed to be overtaken by a groundswell of anger. Irène, Christelle's mother, silent until then, leaped up, waving a finger at her husband's family, shouting, "You're the ones who've done this to Christelle. You're the ones who've attacked us. All this happened because of Papa Léon's death. Because of his notebook!"

These serious accusations left the father's family visibly flabbergasted. Geneviève explained to the astonished medical team that Irène was openly accusing the father's family of having made a witchcraft attack on her daughter. In other words, they wanted to kill Christelle.

Witchcraft in the Democratic Republic of Congo

Witchcraft and sorcery systems in Central Africa serve as an interpretive matrix to explain the world and its disorders, whether they be diseases, unnatural deaths, or any other of life's misfortunes. In 1937, E. E. Evans-Pritchard, in his work on the Azande, attempted to explain the logic of the world of witchcraft, where two main players oppose each other: the *ndoki*, the sorcerer, and the *nganga*, who works to implement the antidote to the work of the *ndoki* (Evans-Pritchard, 1972). The *nganga*, the "master of the secret," is said to have as much power as the *ndoki*, but it is used to protect the community. Any mention of witchcraft inevitably involves both of these role players as well as the complexity of a therapeutic system that is organized to treat the person who has undergone a sorcery attack.

Witchcraft, despite being seemingly antisocial, is probably one of the essential ties that bind Congo society (Nathan and

Lewertowski, 1998). Although it is often considered to be characteristic of uneducated communities, our clinical experience reveals the extent to which interpretations of witchcraft are resorted to in a serious medical situation, quite independently of the social status or level of education of the patients. Anyone interested in the question will be struck by the extent to which people from these ethnic groups, even those who are completely integrated into their host society as immigrants, retain their beliefs in traditional systems, and feel free to consult a traditional healer if they think it necessary.

A serious medical condition—and, what's more, one that the medical world cannot understand—constitutes an incitement to use sorcery as an interpretation. In this particular case, Christelle's weight loss immediately sounded warning bells to her entourage because it could be said to be the pathognomonic[10] sign of a sorcery attack. Although the victim is still alive, they are, in the eyes of all, already dead. Some even say that the victim has been eaten.[11] This was certainly the interpretation Irène made as she watched, helpless, as her daughter wasted away.

Just suggest that there has been an attack of sorcery and immediately family ties will awaken. As everyone knows, beyond the boundaries of the group, there is no protection against the acts of the *ndoki*. Withdrawal from the group means depriving oneself of all possible protection and taking the risk of being designated as an *ndoki* oneself. One might say that whatever procedures are galvanized for treating the affected person, they are all aimed at reintegrating that person into the group.

In Christelle's case, the girl was thought to be the prey of a sorcery attack that was really aimed at her parents. This is the explanation that the family gave us in detail during our encounter. Everything must have started when Papa Léon, Christelle's paternal grandfather, died. This was when his children learned that this respected man, held in awe by all, had chosen Romuald, Christelle's father, to inherit both his authority and his wealth, for Romuald had always held a special place in Papa Léon's family. A brilliant student, he moved to France, where he graduated from the prestigious École des Ponts et Chaussées and began a successful career as an engineer. Everyone agreed that he had made a success of his life. Was that why he thought he could break the rules governing marriage and choose Irène, a Bakongo, for his wife, thereby attracting the wrath of his own family? Romuald remained very close to his father. He regularly sent him money so that he could live decently despite the war that was tearing the Democratic Republic of Congo apart. As soon as he could, Romuald welcomed Papa Léon into his lovely home in the suburbs of Paris. There, pampered by his son, his daughter-in-law, and his grandchildren, he lived out the last two years of his life. While he was still alive, Papa Léon left a notebook to his beloved son, without informing his other children. The notebook was the deed of property to the family compound. It was a choice that transgressed the usual order of things, according to which the eldest son is designated as the heir. For Christelle's mother, it was at this exact moment that her family was attacked and Christelle fell sick. According to the logic of the family, if this hypothesis proved correct, the paternal family held the child's life in their hands.

We turned to Christelle, who is fluent in Lingala. Her sudden sadness led us to understand how close she was to her grandfather and how badly she was still affected by his swift death. In a breaking voice, she told us that since he had died, her parents had argued incessantly. Her tears briefly calmed those in the room. But suddenly, the paternal family counterattacked, now accusing the maternal family of being the cause of the conflicts. We could no longer control the waves of accusations that filled the meeting room that spring afternoon. Curiously, Christelle's father remained silent, shoulders hunched, staring at the floor. The facilitators could no longer make themselves heard, no matter how hard Geneviève tried, in Lingala, to restore calm. Christelle was huddled in her armchair, eyes shut, and breathing with difficulty. Something had to be done quickly. This incendiary outburst had to be extinguished; in the meantime, no further dialogue was possible.

Suddenly, Serge B. sprang from his chair and shouted out to make himself heard, "Enough! What kind of spectacle is this for the medical team? Do you have no respect for them? Who are the heads of family here?"

Two men, older than the others, stood up quickly: Albert, the paternal uncle, and George, a maternal uncle.

Serge B. continued, "This matter is far too grave to be discussed in such a manner. If you, the heads of the families, agree that we must find a solution together, follow me, so that we can continue the discussion in calmer conditions."

There was no need to say another word. Followed by the two elderly uncles, Christelle's physician, and Geneviève, Serge B. walked out to a quiet office nearby.

In the meeting room, the anger was replaced by silence.

No one dared say another word. The outburst had been so violent that everyone was holding their breath, stunned. Christelle stared blankly out of the window. She no longer had the strength to continue weeping as she had at the mention of her grandfather. The members of the medical team look quizzically at Catherine L., hoping she would explain the meaning of what had happened and tell them what was to be done now. While the heads of the families were talking with Serge B. in the other room, Catherine L. explained the scene, emphasizing the seriousness of the accusations. She tried to find the words that would restore some animation to the room, where deathly silence reigned. After she had spoken, a woman with greying hair from the paternal clan stood up and walked toward Christelle's mother. She held her in her arms for a long time. Then, pointing at each of the relatives, ignoring the members of the medical team, she said firmly, "You all know what we must do now in these circumstances." And turning to Christelle, she said, "My girl, I mean you no harm. I want only for you to return home very soon."

She took a glass from the table where a few drinks had been set out. "We each have to come out with what we have to say, once and for all. We have to get the bitterness out of our mouths. We have to say the words to appease this child, so that all this comes to a stop. Because you all heard it," she insisted, "Christelle's life is in danger today."

She went to the sink located in the corner of the room and filled the glass with water. Then, she stood in the center of the circle, turned to Christelle, looked at her for a long time, and lifted the glass to her mouth without drinking the water. She mumbled some words, inaudible to the others, over the glass. The woman was speaking to the water, confiding her doubts, her grudges, and probably her accusations too; she was no doubt also uttering words of reconciliation. Catherine L. realized that a ceremony addressed to Mami Wata,[12] the spirit of the water, was taking place. Christelle's mother went to the paternal relative, took the glass and passed it to her husband, and then to all the other members of the family. The occasion became solemn as each one placed words of anger and appeasement in the water. Christelle's mother was the last to speak to the water divinity.

"Now, do what you have to do!" the aunt ordered Irène.

Irène walked to her daughter. She propped her up a little higher against the pillow. Christelle was now calm. Her mother poured a few drops of water into the palm of her hand. Whispering sacred words, she began washing her child, first her face, wiping her cheeks, then her eyes. She lingered on her forehead; she moved her hands down the neck and on to her chest, murmuring gently all the while. She washed her arms, carefully cleaning her wrists, and then poured the remaining water over the girl's hands, emptying the glass. Then, Irène took her daughter into her arms. Christelle surrendered herself at last to the caresses of her mother. The two were crying.

In the small office nearby, negotiations were in full swing between Serge B., Geneviève, and the two uncles.

Albert turned to Christelle's physician, who had also come into the room. The elder was visibly upset. "First of all, I would like to apologize to you. I'm ashamed of my family's behavior. I don't know what has happened to us."

George, the maternal family head, now spoke, addressing Geneviève directly and avoiding eye contact with Albert. "I would like to apologize to everyone present. I agree with my brother here: nothing can excuse our attitude. We should all be pulling our weight and working together to help Christelle; instead, we are behaving like puppets pulled by the strings of anger and hatred."

Serge B. responded, "Thank you both for your words. It's quite true, I did not understand the anger that was unleashed. I felt that the words were escaping from your mouths quite uncontrollably."

Albert burst out, "It's the *ndoki!*"

The word was uttered. Geneviève immediately seized on it to explain it to the physician, "In our culture, the *ndoki* is both the sorcerer and the action of sorcery itself. Either the sorcerer, or sorcery, uses the power of the invisible, the dead, or the gods, to cast an evil spell on an individual. The *ndoki*'s action is said to be so powerful that it paralyzes any and all attempts to protect or treat the victims. Albert here is certain: the uncontrollable anger that was unleashed earlier is the sign of the influence of sorcery."

The heads of family together confirmed Geneviève's words, which explained the extraordinary outburst of accusations in the other room.

Albert spoke, "The situation is grave. Christelle's life is at stake. The *ndoki* was able to act because her parents are in conflict. Irène did not respect her husband enough." Then, he added with a smile that contrasted with the seriousness of the situation, "But perhaps my nephew has not earned her respect?"

Serge B. responded, "No more accusations now—they are not appropriate. The two families must come together to protect Christelle. She must be protected from the family grudges that let the *ndoki* in. You know how to activate the means of protection customarily used in the two families. Geneviève, what would you do back in your home country in these circumstances?"

Geneviève joined in, "You're right, Serge. The two families must unite, but before that, each member must look at one another. The grudges and disputes must be settled within each family, and only then can they work together."

For the first time that day, George spoke directly to Albert, saying, "I agree with that. We'll do what we would do in our country. After that, I suggest that we go to see the *nganga* together."

Suddenly, Albert was so overcome with emotion that he could not speak. He nodded in acquiescence to George's suggestion. The two heads of family had concluded a veritable pact: they would combine their strength to protect and save Christelle.

All Those Assembled Come Together

Back in the conference room, time seemed to have stood still since Serge B. left with the two uncles. When he returned, serenity and silence reigned. They all took their seats, and Serge B. related the pact that the uncles had concluded; Catherine L. told everyone how the water god had come to appease the families and the child. In addition to the decisions agreed on by those assembled, Christelle had to be helped to pull through her distress over the death of her grandfather. With the agreement of the medical team, we (Serge B. and Catherine L.) suggested that she rapidly begin one-to-one sessions with a psychotherapist. Geneviève would remain in contact with Christelle's family, providing help with their plans and visiting them at their home if necessary. The medical team detailed the treatment program to follow and made an agreement with the families that any examinations that were too invasive would be put on hold unless an emergency arose. With the assent of the surgeons, the surgical procedure scheduled for four days later would be postponed. Lastly, we all agreed to meet again shortly before the summer vacation.

Before concluding this extraordinary encounter, Christelle's maternal uncle once again apologized to the medical team for the family outburst. Speaking for all family members, he thanked them at length for their dedication and the good care provided for his niece. His final words to everyone were conciliatory, "For us, the problems are tied to the marriage of Christelle's parents, because their values are very different from each another's. But there is no guilty party. It's their difference that has created the conflict, not them. From today, our families will come together. We will unite around Christelle and do whatever it takes for the good of the child."

And following words with action, and as if spurred on together, the adults warmly embraced Christelle. Each one, in their own fashion, thanked her for enabling this meeting to happen so that family anger and resentment could finally be appeased.

We had met on a Tuesday afternoon. The next morning, when the medical team made their rounds, they decided not to insert a new central venous catheter. Christelle had begun eating very lightly the previous evening. By the Saturday morning, she was feeling far better and was given permission to spend the weekend at home. A few weeks later, she had gained weight, and her pains had ceased. She left the hospital, never to return.

2
An Angry Man

October 2000

Center for Pain Assessment and Treatment, Adolphe de Rothschild Foundation Hospital, Paris

In attendance: Djibril K., the patient; Dr. Anne Margot-Duclot, the referring hospital practitioner; Ismaël M., native speaker and transcultural mediator; Catherine Lewertowski and Serge Bouznah

First Encounter with Djibril K.

Djibril K. had a reputation for often arriving late—even worse, for forgetting the appointments his physician set for him. He was the sort of patient who annoys his medical team. In fact, the urologist who referred him to the Center for Pain Assessment and Treatment warned his colleague over the phone, "I have no more control over the situation. Monsieur Djibril K. does only what pleases him. He's always late for appointments, he refuses to take our advice, and he no longer follows his treatment plan. He's going to die, and he seems not to care." In the letter he sent with the medical records, the specialist could no longer hide his exasperation with the patient, describing him as "hostile; [he's] a recalcitrant patient who refuses all treatment" despite severe pain in his lower limbs that no one could elucidate. We were forewarned and forearmed—so much so that we had decided to make ourselves comfortable at a table in the cafeteria while we waited for him. But that day, despite all these predictions, Djibril arrived punctually. The paramedics dropped him off at the end of the long hallway leading to the office of the secretary of the Center for Pain, opposite consultation room number 7. Djibril waited for us alone, seated—huddled rather—in his wheelchair, staring ahead mournfully at the yellowing wall whose coat of paint, subjected to the incessant to-ing and fro-ing of stretchers, was peeling. His referring physician had mentioned that usually Djibril dressed soberly, but that day he had donned traditional finery. Beneath his bright orange djellaba, offset by his ebony skin, his broad shoulders, formerly so accustomed to hard work, were now slumped, weighed down by age and ill-health. And as is the case with all paraplegics, at the hips there appeared to be a void. The silky folds of his clothing barely hid his frail, obstinately immobile legs. Djibril clasped his long misshapen hands in his lap. As we passed him in the hallway, and before we had exchanged a single word, we could well imagine how important he considered this encounter with us to be.

Dr. Anne Margot-Duclot, head of the Center for Pain Assessment and Treatment, had been treating Djibril for several months. From the very first consultations, she detected his hostility but could not get to the root of it. She was puzzled by the unusual localization of his pain that no treatment, not even the most advanced, could alleviate. Dr. Margot-Duclot was fully aware that Djibril no longer feared death. Recently, when he had discretely mentioned personal issues, she suggested transcultural mediation. "Your problem is a complicated one. You've been suffering for years, and we haven't managed to give you any relief. Perhaps there are things that we don't understand. Personally, I need the help of colleagues to understand what is happening to you. And, if you prefer, during a mediation session, you can talk in your own language. Perhaps with this approach we will be able to better help you." Djibril immediately agreed to his physician's offer.

We shut the door to the hallway and settled into the consultation room, exchanging a few words in privacy. Then, it was time for Djibril to come in. Dr. Margot-Duclot stood up and walked determinedly to the closed wooden door. There, she knocked twice. We burst out laughing, and only after a few moments did she realize why: opening the door out of her office would lead her into the world of the patient.

We had arranged the chairs in a circle around a coffee table set with cool drinks and coffee. Dr. Margot-Duclot, seated opposite Djibril, opened the thick medical report in a dog-eared cardboard folder in her lap. She had already had recourse to transcultural mediation and knew what was in store: we would have to go through her patient's long, chaotic medical history step by step. We would examine his story to try to grasp it in all its complexity and to give everyone present, Djibril first and foremost, the opportunity to clarify issues hitherto unexplained. As she turned the pages, the physician took us back thirty years.

Djibril was fifty-eight years old at the time of our meeting. He was from Mali, born in the region of Kayes,[1] he specified. It was a region that the transcultural mediator, Ismaël, knew well. Djibril's father was from the Soninke ethnic group, but he was raised, with his many siblings, with the Khassonke.[2] He was twenty-three years old when he arrived in France to join one of his brothers, who had found him a job as a delivery driver with a company in the metropolitan region of Paris. This man of impressive stature quickly adjusted to his new employment. He enjoyed his work and was liked by his colleagues, who appreciated his conscientiousness and good cheer. When we asked him about the first symptoms of his disease, he recounted in Khassonke, the language he had in common with Ismaël, "All of a sudden, at work, I felt very cold. That evening, I asked my wife to warm me up. I was running a high fever. She massaged me, but to no avail. I shivered through the night. The next day, I was so sick I had to be taken to ER, where I was hospitalized."

Djibril clearly remembered that December 7, 1975, a rainy winter's day, when his life changed forever. At the hospital in Paris, the physicians diagnosed an extremely serious case of tubercular meningitis that had already caused extensive neurological damage. After several months of treatment, his tuberculosis was cured, but the cure did not prevent debilitating complications. His lower limbs were partially paralyzed, and he had to use crutches to get around. His first wife, Bintou, walked out on him, leaving their three youngest children in his care. Despite the disease having been successfully treated, he suffered delayed complications three times due to irregular scar tissue, which was compressing the spinal cord. The doctors confirmed a diagnosis of spinal fibrosis.[3]

Dr. Margot-Duclot continued the story, "It was in 1983 that the situation first deteriorated. Djibril had to give up his crutches and use a wheelchair. He underwent many months of treatment in a functional rehabilitation center. Then, life went on, with Djibril coping as best he could until 1996. One morning, his arms were suddenly paralyzed. He was rushed to the hospital, where, it must be said, the surgeons worked miracles: they removed the compression, returning mobility to his arms. The improvement was spectacular, wasn't it?" Djibril nodded in agreement. "We were told that he soon recovered the movement in his hands, but unfortunately his problems did not stop there. Two years later, recurrent urinary infections set in, endangering his life. Such urinary infections are frequent in cases like Djibril's. Their cause is neurological, and they are a result of spinal fibrosis. Without appropriate treatment, patients can die of fulminating septicemia."

The physician explained that in such cases, it is necessary to insert a bladder prosthesis to evacuate stagnant urine and thus reduce the risk of infection. If Djibril was going to agree to this procedure, it would mean permanently wearing a penile sheath to collect his urine. Did he fully understand the implications of the procedure suggested by his urologist? Nothing could be less certain. But he was exhausted by the severity of his disease and ready to agree to anything that would put an end to the humiliating soiling he suffered every day. For the surgeon, the procedure was a success. But for the patient, the postoperative complications were disastrous. Not only did the urinary leakages continue, but Djibril also began suffering extreme pain in his legs, leaving the care staff perplexed. Even worse, he was now impotent. At his instigation, his second wife, Khadija, left him a few months later. And it was in this context that, in 2000, his urologist at the functional rehabilitation center referred Djibril to Dr. Margot Duclot.

"Is It Cured or Will It Continue?"

The man we met for the first time in October 2000 was despondent. It was not anger we initially sensed emanating from the man confined to his wheelchair but rather despair at being soiled day and night by ceaseless urinary leakage. Djibril was profoundly humiliated. After the departure of Khadija, only Sadyo, his youngest child and only daughter, stayed with him. She was the one who prepared his meals every day before going to high school. And as she would shut the door, she would beg her father to take his medical treatment because she sensed that he was giving up the fight. Only a few weeks earlier, Djibril was taking more than twenty pills daily: antidepressants, analgesics, anxiolytics. For the past few days, a nurse had been coming to his home to treat the bedsores that riddled his undernourished skin. He was totally isolated from the rest of his family and from his community. He spent his interminable days within the four walls of his apartment, waiting for Sadyo to return. Only anger seemed to bring him back to life from time to time.

How would we restore hope to this broken man? We were about to spend two hours with Djibril—two hours during which, echoing the account given by his physician, he would be in almost ceaseless dialogue with Ismaël, the transcultural mediator. He reminded us of a parched man who had finally found fresh water to quench his thirst.

Very quickly, Dr. Margot-Duclot helped us launch into an explanation for the reasons for Djibril's anger. She told us, "In 1996, Djibril could no longer use his hands or his arms. An x-ray revealed that he had a syringomyelic cavity. This is a cavity that develops progressively in the spinal cord and compresses the nerve structures. And that explains his symptoms. He underwent surgery: the surgeon inserted a catheter that diverted the liquid that was exerting the pressure, taking it from the cavity to the peritoneum."

Djibril was not entirely fluent in French, nor did he grasp the complex medical terminology of the physician, but he listened attentively. Before we asked Ismaël to translate what had been said, we two facilitators, together with Ismaël, clarified a number of points with the referring specialist.

Serge B. checked with Djibril's physician, "What you're explaining, Anne, is a result of Djibril's tuberculosis?"

"It's a complication."

"Does that mean that the progression of the disease has not been halted—that it's continuing?"

Dr. Margot-Duclot said emphatically, "The tubercular bacterium is dead. He's been cured of his tuberculosis. He's completely cured!"

Djibril, who had remained silent until then, interrupted his physician, surprising us all, "They all told me, just like you're saying now, that I was cured. But look at me today. Am I still a man?" His hands trembled uncontrollably.

Serge B. responded, "We all understand that you are angry, and we need to take the time to understand why." He then turned to the mediator, "Is that clear to you? The tuberculosis was cured because of the antibiotics, but the inflammation continued after that. And it's the inflammation that has caused all these complications. Do you know how we can explain that to Djibril?"

Ismaël said, "That's exactly what I can't translate, even though I understand everything you're saying. In our language, we can't say, 'It's cured, and it continues.'"

Serge B. said, "Could we say that we have treated some of the problem but not the entire problem?"

Dr. Margot-Duclot reacted brusquely, "The tuberculosis is cured. But the body continues to react to the infection, and that's something that medicine is currently not able to treat, nor to prevent."

Ismaël said, "Let me tell you what I understand and then I'll try to interpret for Djibril. What you're saying is that he was sick. You found what he was suffering from, and you treated the problem. But this disease also affected his body, which reacted to it in a certain way . . ."

Dr. Margot-Duclot interrupted Ismaël, "In the nervous system!"

Ismaël, a tad jauntily, responded to her, "Yes, but in our culture, we don't have the concept of a nervous system. For us, it's the body that's concerned. So, I'll tell him that there was a reaction in his body that has given rise to all these problems."

Serge B. summarized, "In fact, the doctors' intervention saved him but could not prevent complications from arising."

Ismaël turned to Djibril and translated the explanations given by his physician.

In the dynamics of a mediation, the physician facilitator and the transcultural mediator rely from start to finish on their respective competences. The physician clarifies the theory and logic underlying the medical treatment, and the mediator provides knowledge of family systems and community resources. Once they have identified the situations where the worlds of the doctor and the patient do not conflict, they work together to establish a framework in which the patient can function comfortably with their own narrative.

In this mediation session, the role of Dr. Margot-Duclot was paramount. By agreeing to open the medical records of her patient, to provide comments on it, and to call into question with us the diagnoses and the therapeutic approach that had been recommended, she was making a clear break with the classic dual relationship in which she alone dealt with the patient, holding the position of expert in her discipline. And even more, by agreeing to questioning by her peers in the presence of the patient—a situation that required all of us to have complete confidence in one another—she was exposing herself to a dynamic of exchanges and reciprocal questioning.

At the outcome of a fruitful discussion, when a meaning that is acceptable to all the protagonists has been negotiated, we can build up a medical narrative over which the patient might be able to take ownership. This narrative is not only made of a literal translation of the physician's account. For the translation to make sense, the theory underlying the medical treatment must be clarified and made accessible to the patient. When this theory is in contradiction with the traditional cultural logic of the patient, we are confronted with semantic dead ends that the mediator will pounce upon. In this case, they centered on the concept of "cure." The concepts we have inherited and the interpretations we make of them are merely "frozen conflicts" (Lévy et al., 2007). It is therefore our duty during the mediation session to repair them, giving them new life.

Ismaël immediately expressed his difficulty in conveying the fact that medical science had eradicated the tuberculosis bacillus but could not prevent the consequences to the spinal cord due to the inflammation, nor the subsequent paraplegia.

"He's been cured of his tuberculosis, but the inflammation continued." Dr. Margot-Duclot hammered home the message. Ismaël knew the Khassonke equivalent of the French *guérir*, to heal or cure, but the assertion that he was supposed to translate, "the patient is cured," seemed incoherent to him, as it implied that the cure was complete, with no complications whatsoever. The explanation given by the physician was in contradiction with the Khassonke conception of a cure: either one is cured, in which case, one is completely cured, or one is not cured. This conception of disorder implies that once the cause of the disorder has been eliminated, the body returns to its condition of integrity.

Through Djibril's sharp reactions during our conversations, we understood that his anger stemmed from the assertion of the doctors that he was cured of his tuberculosis—a declaration made to him in 1976. For him, the appearance of grave complications later flew in the face of what the doctors had already affirmed. From that time onward, the medical team and the patient might well have been on different planets and were, most likely, unaware of the divergencies in their perspective. Twenty-five years after the tuberculosis treatment, when the urologist suggested a surgical procedure on his bladder to prevent urinary infections, a new misunderstanding silently took root in the consultation room. Djibril was expecting one thing only: that he would stop soiling himself daily. The postoperative effects plunged him into deep depression. Not only was the urinary leakage practically permanent, something that had been medically predictable, but he was now impotent. His second wife left him, and that was the final blow. This second misunderstanding reopened the first wound. The anger he had repressed for so many years took over his life.

But now he was able to grasp the clarification we had made. He shared his bitterness with us at length, and then, liberated of a burden that had become too heavy to bear, he revealed a hurt so profound that we were flabbergasted. As he revealed the root causes of his sadness, this simple man, so deeply religious, told us with great decorum of the indescribable shame that gnawed away at him day and night: because he soiled himself, he could no longer pray. How could he come before God when his body was impure? That was the essential question that Djibril asked us, that day in October 2000. It is a question that concerned not only him but all Muslim patients who must face the same situation. We were not yet able to answer him. Before we could do so, we would have to continue our long journey together.

Tracking Down Misapprehensions

Because certain immigrant patients are not fluent in the language of their healthcare workers, physicians often consider that the linguistic issue is the only obstacle in the treatment plan. They call on the services of an interpreter, hoping to resolve the problem. But what do the interpreters do? At the request of the physician, they translate—that is, they *re*tell the information to be shared with the patient in another language. In these situations, the interpreter is at the service of the medical staff. Interpreters make the adaptations that are possible for them in response to what the medical profession asks of them, and will hesitate to question the physicians if, by any chance, the concepts to be interpreted have no corresponding terms in the patient's language. In such cases, the interpreters often decide on their own to suggest a particular word or turn of phrase that they think is close in meaning; the physician cannot call the translation into question.

Misunderstandings and even errors of interpretation may arise from such lack of precision. If by chance the interpreter wishes to discuss this difficulty with the physician, the customary organization of the consultation and the rhythm at which the physician has to work—ten to twenty patients per half-day—makes any such dialogue virtually impossible. And so, face to face with a physician who has no choice but to get to the core of the matter, the patient, out of courtesy, feigns understanding, and might even give the impression that there is no need for an interpreter.

Second Extract

Catherine L. wondered out loud, "Did Djibril inform his family back home when he was rushed to the emergency room? Did they say anything there about all the misfortunes that he suffered?"

Ismaël translated the question and recounted Djibril's response to the group. "Djibril has explained that of course his mother consulted a marabout—a *mori*.[4] But he did not want to pay attention to what was said in Mali. His mother tried to insist that he take the healer's prescription, but he answered, 'The whites were strong enough to save me. Why do you want me to look for solutions elsewhere?'"

Catherine L., grasping Djibril's resistance to traditional healing, returned to Ismael, "I hear what Djibril is saying, and I respect his attitude, but all the same, I'd like to know if, at the time, the *mori* explained to his mother why her eldest son had been affected."

A long dialogue in Khassonke between Djibril and Ismaël ensued, and then Ismaël resumed the conversation, "Yes, the *mori* did indeed provide an explanation. He spoke of a spell. Djibril himself has told me that very early on, he had some intuition as to the origin of the attack. In his opinion, it was all tied to his first marriage. His first wife was desired by four suitors. It was Djibril who won her over, to the great displeasure of one of his rivals, who, one evening, threatened him in public, 'If you take this woman for your wife, you'll never have any peace.' And do you know what Djibril answered him? 'You are not God!' Two of the suitors are already dead. Despite all this, Djibril had five children with Bintou, all boys. When his medical condition worsened, his wife left him. Djibril returned to Mali and took a second wife, Khadija. After the wedding ceremony, his brother advised him to consult a traditional healer to obtain the protection he required. He was already badly handicapped, but he refused. Khadija bore him three children, two sons and a daughter."

Djibril's obstinate refusal to follow the repeated advice from his mother and brother, thus cutting himself off from his family and community networks, raised questions for us. Despite the initial misunderstanding concerning his cure, Djibril retained his confidence in the Western medicine that had saved his life. But this was not sufficient an explanation in our eyes. Djibril's solitude struck us from the first moments of our encounter when we saw him, alone, in the hallway of the Center for Pain Assessment. Why was this man, a member of a large family clan, not accompanied by his family members?

Our next step was to talk at length about the memory of his father. At this stage, Ismaël's skills were indispensable in helping us weave together a meaningful narrative using a few sparse but complex elements of Djibril's life.

And this is what we learned: Djibril's father was a Soninka who, for reasons unknown, had left his group to join a Khassonke village. The Khassonke live in close proximity to the Soninka, but the two ethnic groups are distinct. Ismaël explained that migrating from the Soninka to the Khassonke was a rare occurrence; it might have been more like an exile triggered by a serious conflict in the group of origin. The reasons for this exile were no doubt somehow related to the radical choices Djibril's father made: he abandoned the traditional Soninka practices to adopt a far stricter form of the Muslim religion. He married a Khassonke woman, Djibril's mother, who continued practicing the traditional Khassonke way of life with its fetishes and healers. As a result, Djibril was raised between two extremes: Islam on the one hand, embodied by a father he adored and to whom he was very close, and the traditional animist practices of his mother's family. Out of loyalty to his father, a very religious man, well-read in the tenets of his faith, who refused anything outside the realm of Islam, Djibril was always very distrustful of animist customs. Although he did not question the validity of the interpretations of the various *mori* his family members met, he refused to follow their advice. Thus, he gradually cut himself off from his family network—a very active one—limiting himself to managing his problems exclusively using Western medicine, which he considered to be more efficacious.

Ismaël took up the narrative. "Now Djibril has recounted a very important story about his father. It's a story, I believe, that will help us better grasp what has happened to him. One day, his father invited all of his daughters to a meal that lasted late into the night. Since he could not let them go home alone, he decided to accompany each one back to her husband. As he was returning home, a jinn blocked his path. Seeing Dr. Margot-Duclot's surprise, Ismaël gave an explanation: jinn are the spirits that live in the bush and in the backwaters. They are mythical beings who are considered to be the true owners of the earth. The villagers said that Djibril's father refused to turn around: he confronted the jinn and then continued on his way. But when he reached home, he collapsed. He never said another word and remained paralyzed for two difficult years. After that, he died.

After a lengthy discussion about tubercular meningitis, four of the attendees—three physicians and the transcultural mediator—were continuing a serious conversation with the patient about other interpretations of his illness. These new, seemingly incongruous cultural points of view within the hospital setting were suddenly possible now that the physician had clearly stated, in the presence of the patient, that Western medical treatment had its limitations.

The first interpretation that emerged tied the origin of the illness to the sorcery attack instigated by one of the rejected rivals for the hand of Djibril's first wife. The cause of the disorder apparently lay in the very process of the union entered into between the two families. According to this hypothesis, Djibril's illness meant that the entire clan of his family should examine the terms of the alliance; they would have to undertake a meticulous verification to see whether the indispensable ritual forms of protection to ensure fertility, health, and wealth had been respected. The second interpretation involved the death of Djibril's father. The family at the time unhesitatingly incriminated an attack by jinn, the invisible beings that inhabit a world parallel to that of humans. According to Khassonke and Soninka myths, still prevalent, it is said that jinn may make alliances with humans. In exchange for the wealth or the fertility of a clan, humans undertake, often over many generations, to pay regular tribute to the jinn in the form of sacrifices and offerings. Should these offerings cease for one reason or another, the jinn are said take revenge on the humans, afflicting them with endless ills. It should be recalled that the arrival of Islam in the eleventh century overturned the subtle balance between the world of humans and that of the invisible creatures; the faithful were required to abandon their age-old practices and customs.

After a lengthy discussion during which Djibril and Ismaël went over the chronology and circumstances of the events that had been related, dissecting and analyzing the details, they agreed that the illness and all the misfortunes with which Djibril had been afflicted since 1975 were consistent with the same logic as the death of his father: they were the consequence of a transgression of the alliance with the jinn.

Catherine L. and Serge B. summarized all the elements of this story in order to put forward a suggestion to the group and to Djibril.

At last Serge B. said, "What strikes me in Djibril's account is a constant feature: each time some form of wealth comes his way, there's a danger associated with it. When he married his wife, she gave him five sons, but underlying that was a threat of death. When he came to France, he quickly found work, but he fell ill. The same was true for his father: when he converted to Islam and gave up his traditions, the jinn manifested themselves. I wonder if the question that is asked of Djibril is not the following: how to retain wealth and at the same time protect yourself from danger? And the more I wonder, the more I think that it concerns not only Djibril, but also his children. It is thus a crucial question for him as well as for his entire family."

Djibril trembled at these words. Ismaël, sensing his tension, took the time necessary to explain what Serge had said, deploying all the subtlety of his native language. Djibril's attitude changed visibly. Suddenly, he seemed very worried. Hesitating, he glanced enquiringly at Ismaël several times. The mediator asked him to share his preoccupation with us. After a long silence, during which he seemed to be struggling with his emotions, Djibril told us that his first grandson, born prematurely a few weeks earlier, was, that very moment, hovering between life and death in the neonatal intensive care unit of a hospital in Paris.

The grandson's name was Djibril.

The information divulged by the patient at that instant was the missing piece of the puzzle. It enabled us to see the story of a man within the context of a transgenerational family narrative. If we examined all the elements, we now knew in the light of the interpretation negotiated between Djibril and Ismaël what transpired was that it was always the male firstborn who was attacked by the jinn. Djibril had made exactly the same connection, and his unease provided confirmation of the group's hypothesis. For him, at that very moment, there was no other possible alternative. His rank as head of the family and the eldest of his brothers meant that it was he who, crucially, had to take action: he had to make amends for the transgression so that the attacks would cease. He knew he could not act alone; he had to contact his family in Mali to activate all the means of protection necessary.

What did we construct together? We had produced a new definition of Djibril's medical condition, tying the patient's illness to the vision of the "disease" as seen by the doctors in a construct that was not exclusively biomedical, nor totally Khassonke, but which took something from both worlds to offer a new narrative that would give meaning to the sudden appearance of illness in the life of this patient. This type of transcultural mediation has an astonishingly motivating effect and makes it necessary for both the patient and the physician to change perspective completely. Illness was no longer an event with no meaning in Djibril's life; it had become an essential element of information concerning the very meaning of his existence. It meant that he had to emerge from his solitude to take action—action aimed at protecting not only himself but also his children and grandchildren. Thus, Djibril finally took on an active role in the eyes not only of his family but also of the entire Khassonke group.

The handicapped patient—the angry, humiliated man who was ready to give up everything—suddenly took his rightful place as head of the family, becoming the protector of his lineage.

Three months had passed since our first encounter. Again, we met at the Fondation Rothschild. Djibril arrived punctually, this time accompanied by his daughter Sadyo. It was immediately obvious to us that he was better. He was taking his medication and no longer complained of pain.

We anxiously awaited the arrival of Ismaël, who had gone to Mali, sent there by his university. Ismaël had told us that he would ask the Great Imam of Bamako for advice. The Imam was a highly respected man in Mali, and he was expected to give an answer to the theological question Djibril was asking: How can one pray when the body is impure?

Ismaël told us, "I managed to meet with the Imam. I explained what we were doing here at the Fondation Rothschild. I transmitted Djibril's question to him, and today I can give you the answer. It shines a brilliant light on the problem: 'To pray, it is enough for the believer's heart to remain pure.'"

Two weeks later, Djibril invited his eight children to a sumptuous traditional meal to celebrate his return, at last, into the Muslim world. Ismaël attended too.

3

If You're a Human Being, Change Your Skin Immediately!

August 2009

A consultation room in the dermatology department of Hôpital Necker Enfants Malades, Paris

In attendance: Alice and Pierre M., the parents; Dr. V., the hospital physician, a dermatologist; Robert, the transcultural mediator; Catherine Lewertowski and Serge Bouznah

First Encounter with the M. Family

Six chairs were arranged in a circle, as we had requested, and there was little space remaining in this dim, narrow consultation room. It was hot outside; we waited patiently for the M. family to arrive—they had warned us that they would be a few minutes late. Everyone present was aware of the tragedy that had struck the parents once again. Their son, barely two months old, was dying—soon to be the fourth death out of six children. What parents could bear such pain? When Alice M. finally entered the room with her husband, Pierre, the anxiety was visible on her face. Despite the grave condition of their son, the couple appeared calm and smiled reservedly at each of us as we greeted them. Pierre sat down next to his wife. He was about thirty years old, short, dry, wiry, with a friendly face, and attired in a tracksuit. Alice wore a green and yellow boubou, a traditional dress of West and Central Africa; her belly still showed the roundness of her recent pregnancy. Sitting tall and straight next to her husband, she was by far the taller and more corpulent of the two. The couple seemed tied together by their combat and their sadness.

The dermatologist who had been treating the family's children for several years had requested a transcultural mediation session so that he could understand the incomprehensible: the reason why the mother had refused a therapeutic abortion, although she was fully aware that the child she was bearing was carrying a fatal genetic disease. Since the child's birth, she had shown no interest whatsoever in the baby. The physicians had already informed the family that their baby would die. It was a matter of weeks, perhaps only days. Despite the prognosis, Alice still refused to see her son, to touch him, or even to give him a name. The medical team was used to dealing with extremely complex cases, but her behavior so disconcerted them that they did not know how to deal with it.

Dr. V. had already explained to the couple that during the meeting with our mediation team that afternoon, we would spend as much time as was needed to understand the issues. He made it clear that he would be present with them throughout this very different type of consultation; it might take two hours, perhaps longer. Alice and Pierre were extremely grateful that we had all made ourselves available for such an unusually long time; the planned duration underlined how important it was for their physician to understand their situation. The family members seemed perfectly aware of the exceptional nature of this encounter, and this might have explained why Alice clearly expressed her fears from the outset. Before the hospital physician could begin explaining the medical situation, she started off in perfect French, openly expressing her doubts and her questions.

"Dr. V. has been helping us a great deal, but I must be frank with you. I keep wondering if you are not hiding something from me. Am I solely responsible for whatever has been striking my children?"

Alice stared intently at each of the participants. She was expecting this meeting to provide the answers to the questions that had been haunting her for the past five years. Why her? Why her children? Why so many of them?

An Extremely Rare Genetic Disease

Alice and her husband are from the former Republic of Zaïre (since 1997, the Democratic Republic of Congo [DRC]) and belong to the Bakongo[1] ethnic group. Pierre arrived in France in 1992, and Alice joined him in 2000. Six children, all boys, were born to the couple. Three of their children had already died, and the prognosis for the newborn baby was grim. The dermatologist had already met with the couple frequently to discuss their children's disease. Nevertheless, we devoted much of this first encounter to explaining the medical hypotheses that led to the diagnosis of an extremely rare genetic disease. Despite their emotional suffering and the complexity of the concepts used, the couple listened attentively to the explanations given by Dr. V. When our turn came, we also probed these explanations, our objective being to shed light for the couple on the notion of a genetic disease, the role of chromosomes and genes, genetic inheritance and transmission, and the role of gametes.[2]

The couple's life in France had got off to a fine start when Jeremiah was born in 2003. Just think, their firstborn was a son, and one who weighed in at more than eight pounds and measured twenty-one inches![3] Alice did not mask her pride. By the time of our encounter, Jeremiah was a fine young boy who was about to start school. In 2005, when Alice got pregnant again, this time with male twins, the family was delighted, and the pregnancy went smoothly. As soon as the boys were delivered in a hospital in the Paris area, the doctors diagnosed them with an extremely serious dermatological disease. They were born completely hairless—no eyebrows, no hair—and with no foreskin. The babies looked strangely like old men.[4] On their very first day of life, their epidermis thickened, became infected, and cracked. The twins were soon suffering from cutaneous infections, complicated by extremely severe septicemia. They could barely take any nourishment, and their general condition worsened daily. Marc was the first to die, at six weeks. Nathan was then transferred for diagnosis and specialized treatment to the pediatric dermatology department of the hospital where we were meeting. This was where the family met the dermatologist who continued to treat Nathan.

At this point of the narration, Alice looked down and clenched her hands on her colorful skirt. Tears came to her eyes. Silently, Pierre handed a tissue to his wife. The dermatologist continued his narration. Diagnosing Nathan proved complex, and he was examined over several weeks. The physicians took various samples and conducted analyses. Finally, they reached their conclusion. The twins had been born with an extremely rare genetic disease[5] of which only 150 cases have been reported worldwide. The gene involved was known. Despite intensive care at the hospital, Nathan died of septicemia at the age of five months.

As always in the case of a genetic disease, the M.'s family history was investigated. A molecular analysis showed a mutation in the gene responsible for the disease. However, this gene mutation was not found in either parent. There was another plausible and rare hypothesis: a parental germline mosaicism—that is, a mutation present only in some of the sex cells or gametes of either parents. If this hypothesis was validated, it would mean the pathology of the couple's children was even rarer. Just like for all diseases of this type, each new pregnancy is subject to unknown factors. For Alice and Pierre, the risk appeared low. If Alice were to get pregnant again, only amniocentesis[6] would determine if the fetus was affected, and the parents would then be able to decide, depending on the results, whether to agree to a therapeutic termination.

In 2006, Alice gave birth to a healthy baby whom they named Joshua. Sadly, during her following pregnancy, no amniocentesis was practiced for reasons that are unclear (she may have made her appointment too late). Samuel was born in 2008 with the genetic disease. Alice had shown strong maternal feelings for Joshua, but she refused to see Samuel, despite the urging of the hospital team.

Samuel died two months later in intensive care. And so, when Alice once again became pregnant late in 2008, the dermatologist and his team provided strong support for the seemingly ill-fated couple. An amniocentesis carried out in the fourth month of pregnancy showed that the child was affected. Yet, to the surprise of the entire medical team, who now knew the family well, Alice refused to have the pregnancy terminated.

Dr. V. said, "We wondered if she refused because of religious reasons—the family are active members of an evangelical church."

The medical team took cognizance of the couple's decision and respected it, admiring the courage of the parents for carrying an unborn child who would certainly suffer from the same genetic disease as its siblings. Everyone knew that the child would die quickly. Labor set in early in July and proved particularly long and painful: the baby was in breech position. The newborn boy had the same appearance as his brothers with the disease, and he quickly developed the same infectious complications. The prognosis was grim, with a life expectancy of barely a few months. From the moment he was born, Alice refused to look at or touch her child, behaving exactly as she had with Samuel. Her husband chose the name for the boy: Élie.

Interpreting the mother's disconcerting attitude was problematic. How could the team accept the fact that she ignored her dying child? They were utterly perplexed, and the team's lack of comprehension risked compromising their ability to provide calm, balanced support to the family.

Alice and Her Husband's Explanations: A Desperate Search for Meaning

In the small office, Alice took her turn to speak. Her husband remained on the sidelines, allowing her to recount their ordeal. When she was overcome with emotion, he leaned toward her, gently touching her arm. Alice apologized in advance for what she was about to say. She knew that the physician would most likely be shocked by what she would divulge. But today, her first meeting with us, she felt that she had permission to talk of what had remained secret, or at least confined to the family circle until then.

Alice said, "It all started when the twins were born in 2005. When we saw them, my husband and I didn't need to exchange a word. We knew immediately that they were different. Their faces, their wrinkled skin, the absence of hair on their heads and bodies were all signs that terrified us."

Catherine L. seized on the word. "Different? Do you mean that you wondered about the nature of the children? Did you wonder where they came from?"

The parents nodded in agreement.

Catherine L. called on the mediator. "Robert, I know that in your culture, the birth of a child is always a message to be deciphered. When Alice tells us that she and Pierre were frightened, do you think that they wondered if their children were really human beings?"

Robert answered with no hesitation, "Perhaps they even thought that they were spirits, or ancestors returning to their home."

Dr. V. had no time to express his astonishment before Alice and Pierre confirmed in unison, "Yes, those are exactly the questions we asked."

Alice then told us how, the day after the birth, crushed, she called her mother in DRC. There, a family meeting was quickly called: they all knew that it was urgent to solve the question raised by the birth of the children. Who were they? Where did they come from? What message did they bear? The family members were divided on what advice to give the parents in the case of these twins. Should they be retained in the world of humans or be allowed to return to their own world, the world of spirits?

It was an impossible dilemma. The physical appearance of the children tied them to their ancestors. But the family knew that a person with evil intentions can use witchcraft to manipulate "twin spirits" to attack a family. The question was so complex that it could not be resolved rapidly. In Paris, Alice and her husband were waiting, in a state of deep indecision and distress. The doctors, in close contact with the couple, attempted in vain to save Marc and Nathan. While the treatment was in progress, the family back in DRC asked Alice to respect the traditional funeral rites if the children were to die; everything should be done according to the rules.

When Joshua was born one year later in perfect health, both parents and doctors were thankful. The parents knew that they had followed the rites of their native country, and the doctors were reassured. Statistically, the births of the other affected boys were explained as extremely rare cases of the transmission of a genetic mutation in the family. But the birth of Samuel in 2008 struck everyone like a bolt of lightning.

In appearance, Samuel was identical to the twins. Once again, the family in DRC rallied to find out why the couple was again struck with such a grave misfortune. Given the seriousness of the situation, the families of both mother and father decided to call on the local healer, the *nganga*. His verdict: the family was the victim of a sorcery attack. The twins were spirits that were manipulated by a sorcerer with evil intentions. If they were not "anchored" in their world—by being treated in the traditional way—they would return yet again. Alice's mother was tasked with giving the message to her daughter. This is what she said, as related by Alice:

"You should never have allowed yourself to become attached to the twins. The doctors should not have treated them. Doing so meant that you encouraged them to return to your home. The child who has just been born is one of the twins who has returned. Now, if you want him to leave, you must not see him, must not touch him, and must not give him a name. Show no interest in him. Consider him a stranger until he dies. When he dies, have him buried facing downward. Most importantly, give him a mark: cut him or break a finger, the way we do here, so that you can recognize him if he comes back again. Use strong words to talk to him, so that he never returns, and leave him without ever visiting his tomb again."

Alice followed her mother's instructions to the letter while her husband liaised with the medical team. When Samuel died, Pierre organized the burial, respecting the prescribed ritual as far as possible. However, the traditional plants on which to lay the body of the child had still not arrived from DRC. Despite this obstacle, Pierre organized the funeral and, for want of the help he needed for the occasion, did not give the child a "mark."

Alice once again became pregnant, this time with Élie, late in 2008. Amniocentesis showed that the child was affected with the genetic disease, but after consulting her mother, Alice followed her advice and refused to have her pregnancy terminated.

Alice's mother instructed her, "You must refuse an abortion: this is the second twin who is returning. You must 'anchor' him. Tie him to his world, as you did for the first one. Allow him to be born and then do everything you can so that you prevent him from ever coming back again."

And that was why Alice did not have an abortion early: not because of their Christian beliefs, as the medical team had believed, but because it was imperative that the body of the child be given the traditional rites so that he would never return. It is difficult to grasp the extent of the young mother's misery and fear during the last months of her pregnancy. Even worse, the *nganga* consulted by the family back in DRC had mentioned a possibility that did not bode well, saying, "It's a good thing that no one in your own family wishes your daughter any evil. With the beings she has carried, she would already be dead!"

Alice feared that the child she was carrying would be the death of her too. When, after Élie's birth, she avoided looking at the baby, she sensed the incomprehension, the hostility, even, of certain members of the hospital staff. That day, at our encounter, she was able to talk about it, and she was brimming with emotion. She said, "I couldn't tell them anything. Who would have understood what my mother told me to do?"

Since she wanted to avoid all contact with her son, it was her husband who named the child. As a faithful member of his evangelical church, he chose the name "Élie" in honor of the prophet Elijah—an emblematic figure in the three monotheistic religions, capable of raising the dead, and chased from his land for trying to impose the worship of a single God. Pierre dissolved into tears when we discussed the destiny of the prophet during our session. The dermatologist still remembered when Pierre, numb with pain, had asked permission to wash his child with holy water. The dermatologist agreed. How could he stop Pierre, a man torn between his Christian beliefs and the interpretation of the *nganga* in his home country, from making this last-ditch attempt to save his son?

The Anthropological Background: The Child Messenger

In the worldview of the Bakongo, that of Alice and Pierre, the birth of every child constitutes an enigma for the family to solve. The child is, first of all, a stranger who must be welcomed into the family; the family must then decode the message they bear. When a child is born, the family tries to answer two questions: Who is this child? What message do they bring to us?

Unlike Western psychological conceptions centered on the notion of the autonomous subject, the Bakongo consider the child first and foremost as a being who links two seemingly disconnected worlds (Nathan, 1985). The child establishes a link between the paternal and maternal lineages, naturally. It connects the world of the living with both the world of the dead and the world of the ancestors, the protecting spirits of the lineage. In this society, twins (*maphasa*) are generally considered as mysterious beings in possession of many powers and close to the spirits. The arrival of twins in a family will throw the life of their community into disarray. The Bakongo consider twins to be sacred children (*bana banlongo*), and they are said to select the family in which they will live (di Mbumba, 2005). The Bakongo know that twins must be treated carefully because at any moment they may leave their parents to return to where they came from—the world of the spirits. And so, they are the object of particular attention. To retain them in the world of the living, families must organize a strictly codified ritual to convince them that they are fully fledged members of the clan. Nevertheless, the community is wary of twins, who have the power to harm whomever they wish.

In such a belief system, the illness of a child is interpreted as yet another message destined for the entire group of which the child is a member. This is even more valid in the case of twins. The *nganga*, the traditional healer who is usually consulted, must identify and then modify any discord existing between family members, the ancestors, the spirits, and the dead. Flawed interactions between these entities are thought to explain the disorder that has come about in the family—in this case, an illness.

After Samuel's birth in 2008, the *nganga* in DRC consulted by the family diagnosed the situation as an attack perpetrated by a sorcerer (*ndoki*). According to Bakongo tradition, a sorcerer's action involves three players: the person who emits the attack (the sorcerer), an intermediate being (an ancestor or a spirit instrumentalized by the sorcerer), and a target (the group or an individual). In this case, the twins, considered to be spirits, were identified as the vector used by the sorcerer to destroy the M. couple. The nature of the attack—the manipulation of spirits—was very serious because it affected the couple's fertility. The *nganga* specified that the attack came from a member of the family, thus opening up an extremely dynamic process of questioning among family members. The clans of both the mother and the father of the children came together, hoping to find answers as quickly as possible to put an end to the attack. This would ensure that Alice, her husband, and their children would be protected from then on.

The two questions that underpinned the discussions among the family groups, both in DRC and in France, were: Why? and Who? These family discussions used the same strategy we employed during our initial mediation session, when we discussed the M. family and their matrimonial history. Each participant sought the "breach"—the "opening" through which an attack could infiltrate the family. Questions relating to the union between Alice and her husband provided us with the essential clues. They had met in Kinshasa,[7] outside the framework of a family arrangement. They did not organize a traditional marriage ceremony. In this case, the lack of a traditional marriage may have been the "opening" for a sorcery attack. No bridewealth was given for Alice. Not giving any bridewealth is very serious indeed. It constitutes a transgression of the basic rules of the alliance and thus nullifies the marriage. Was this the reason for the children's condition? Alice and her husband discussed this issue quite openly. They had long been aware of the need to formalize their union as soon as possible.

Let us give some additional details concerning the Bakongo kinship system, which is worth taking into consideration here. It is composed of basic social cells, which include both the couple's extended family and the clan. Traditional marriage, even more than civil marriage, is of fundamental importance: more than uniting two people, it unites two clans. The bridewealth that is exchanged is the formal symbol of the alliance between the two families concerned. From a sociological perspective, bridewealth is compensation to the matrilineal clan for the void created when a young woman leaves her clan for that of her future husband. The giving of bridewealth is the visible part of a transaction that is more than the transmission of goods; it generates numerous negotiations between the families, providing opportunities for them to become acquainted and to identify one another prior to the union. Bridewealth negotiations enable the families to pinpoint possible incompatibilities, for example an illness suffered by one of the future spouses, the presence of other aspiring suitors (or brides), an obscure past, or unexplained deaths in either family. It is only after these negotiations are completed that the union will be blessed. The blessing offers traditional forms of protection that will reinforce the marriage, enabling the couple to exhibit their prosperity by producing healthy children who will contribute to the wealth of the entire clan. In Bakongo cultural logic, bridewealth cannot be reduced to a simple transaction. The process of creating an alliance reconsolidates the foundations of the whole group and functions as a plea to the ancestors of the two clans to protect the couple and ensure their fertility.

In the DRC of today, many young men and their families do not have the means to respect the obligations of gift giving and the other transactions that allow an official marriage to take place.

Those old enough to start a family often find ways of sidestepping the dictate. For example, a couple may begin by living together (this was the case of the M. couple), have children, and present them to their families as a fait accompli, thus avoiding the cycle of gift giving that is a necessary part of the creation of a formal alliance between families. However, such practices open the door to family conflicts and accusations of sorcery, particularly in urban environments, where the tradition has resonance (Dekens, 2007).

Alice and Pierre are from a region where matrilineal kinship is dominant: children are considered as part of the maternal lineage, as we indicated in the story of Christelle. This also signifies that property, family names, and hereditary rank and titles are all transmitted through the female line. The maternal uncle acts as the head of the clan: he holds authority over the children and transmits his inheritance to them. The husband, even though he is the biological father, plays a secondary role because he does not belong to his wife's clan group.

Alice and her husband agreed that their failure to hold a traditional marriage may have aroused the anger of Alice's maternal clan, in particular some of her maternal aunts, whom she mentioned by name. Did these women think that by exempting himself from a traditional marriage, Pierre was trying to claim the children for himself? At this stage of our meeting, both agreed that it was urgent to legitimize their marital status and pay the bridewealth.

October 2009
A consultation room in the pediatric dermatology service in Paris
    Second meeting with Alice and Pierre M.

Élie had died only a few days earlier in the neonatal unit. Our first encounter with the M. family had been so enriching and had shed so much light on the questions raised by the dermatologist and his team that after the death of the child, and at the request of Alice and Pierre, he arranged another session with us.

This time, no fear was palpable. When Alice and her husband entered the consultation room, despite the tragedy that had just struck them, some measure of calm was visible on their saddened faces. Alice immediately launched into an explanation of what had transpired since our first meeting.

"When we came out of our meeting in August, after telling you so much, sharing so many important things with you, I asked my husband to give me the strength to see the child. I wanted to talk to him, to pronounce, at last, my mother's words. Pierre came with me, and I went into the ward. I was scared. I leaned over the bed and said to the child, 'Stop persecuting us. We don't want you. You have been three times; you have gone three times. If you are a human being, change your skin immediately! If not, return to where you came from. You have no business with us.'"

Two days later, the medical team informed the family that Élie had died.

After that, the couple decided to protect themselves by avoiding a new pregnancy, which could engender jealousy and trigger yet another sorcery attack. Soon after, we were informed that Alice had temporarily moved out of her family home; furthermore, she was using a contraceptive patch. Both husband and wife were convinced that, given the seriousness of the situation, they should return to DRC as soon as they could to carry out the traditional treatment for purification and protection. And in fact, Pierre soon contacted his family to prepare his return.

Alice told her doctor that if she became pregnant again within the following year and the child was affected, she would agree to have her pregnancy terminated. The couple also agreed to an appropriate form of therapy to help them through their unique process of bereavement.

To bury Élie, Pierre waited more than three weeks for the traditional burial plants to arrive from his country, creating an additional complication for the hospital. Nevertheless, the staff continued to support the family's decision. This time, Pierre had organized matters so that he had the help he needed to hold the funeral in full accordance with Bakongo ritual funeral requirements.

4

Who Will Carry the Parasol for Me?

February 2010
Center for Pain Assessment and Treatment, Fondation Adolphe de Rothschild, Paris

In attendance: Moncef, the patient; Dr. Anne Margot-Duclot, the referring hospital practitioner; Leila Oudrhiri, the transcultural mediator; Catherine Lewertowski and Serge Bouznah

Second Encounter with Moncef

Leila O., the transcultural mediator, addressed the moderators: "A few days ago, I had a long conversation with Moncef's wife, as you asked me to do after our first meeting. Her husband told her I'd be contacting her, and she was anxiously awaiting my call. She wanted to know why we were talking about matters concerning their home country and the family—the issue here was a surgical procedure. I explained how we work and why we needed her to be present. She apologized for not being able to attend today, again, but promised that next time she would come to help her husband. She told me that since he had fallen sick, things were very difficult at home. He gets very bad-tempered and often shouts at her and the children, coming out with hurtful words that he cannot control. Lately, she has even become frightened. She no longer recognizes the man she married—a man who used to be so strong, so calm. And that was when she spoke of the *shour*. . . ."

Three Weeks Previously

The department secretary had already showed him into the doctor's consulting room. Moncef was waiting for us, his back turned to the door. As we came in, we might have thought he had fallen asleep, leaning on the crutch that he would cling to throughout the session. When we came in, he laboriously raised his chest to greet us. He mumbled a *bonjour*, giving us the impression that he was awakening from a long sleep and no longer quite knew in which world he had emerged. This was Moncef, the finest cabinet maker in his neighborhood. This was the man who had spent countless hours repairing, sanding, planing, and assembling his works in the oak and ash wood of which he was so fond. Until that day in October—at exactly 11 A.M., for Moncef had just looked at the large clock above his workbench—when he suddenly fell to his knees for no reason he could understand, overcome by a mysterious affliction.

Moncef began, "I was extremely frightened. I fell so suddenly! I could not move, could not get up. My workers had to carry me to my car to take me home."

Until that day, Moncef had led a quiet life untroubled by health issues. He had just celebrated his fiftieth birthday with his wife and two sons, aged eight and ten. He was well liked, even if he did not find it easy to make friends. He was born in Tunisia, where he spent his childhood in a small town near Bizerte, a place he regularly returned to on vacation. Of course, since he had settled in France nearly thirty years earlier, life had not always been easy, but he made a success of his career as a cabinetmaker, and it was work he was passionate about. He married Fatima, a woman he loved and whom he respected profoundly. But alas, he said, there had previously been another woman whom he had first met when he arrived in Paris. They only lived together briefly, but long enough for her to bear him a daughter. His passion for this woman waned as quickly as it fired up, and the separation was painful, with much quarreling and many rebukes. The conflictual situation subsided with time, and Moncef was able to see his daughter again. Many years later, he started a new life with Fatima. He lacked nothing and thanked God every day for the way his life had turned out, until that collapse. . . .

Dr. Margot-Duclot spoke, "This accident triggered a whole series of problems for Moncef. He was initially hospitalized in emergency care and diagnosed with spinal cord compression by osteoarthritis. He asked me many questions about his condition, wanting to know how long it had been present in his body. I explained that it was a process of wear, with deterioration of the bony tissue by osteoarthritis that sets in insidiously. I explained that medicine could have no real effect on it. In Moncef, this phenomenon caused a narrowing of the spinal cervical canal with a compression of the spinal cord. That explained why his lower limbs were so suddenly paralyzed."

Moncef, staring into space, spoke softly, "I could not understand why that happened to me out of the blue, because I had never been sick before. The hospital physician really scared me. He told me that I had to undergo surgery very soon, otherwise I'd be paralyzed and confined to a wheelchair for the rest of my life."

Dr. Margot-Duclot recounted, "Initially, the surgeon thought that he would operate only on the herniated disk,[1] but because of the compression, the procedure was far more complex, involving what we call a laminectomy. This procedure involves freeing the spinal cord by widening the spinal canal. It is not risk free because the spinal cord may be made fragile by the compression. There is a risk that the neurological symptoms may be aggravated."

Moncef interrupted, "I remember that before the operation, I was so scared, I couldn't sleep. I smoked cigarette after cigarette. . . ."

Dr. Margot-Duclot picked up her narrative. "Fortunately for Moncef, the surgery was successful. He quickly regained movement of his legs, but then debilitating pains set in, affecting his arms and legs. What was incomprehensible was that they were more severe than before the procedure. Nothing we did could relieve Moncef of his pains. He was extremely tired and lost nearly thirty pounds[2] in just a few weeks. All these symptoms could not be related to the postoperative effects. There had to be something else. I ran the full range of tests on him, and then—and I remember it very well, it was a late Friday afternoon—I was doing my rounds. I saw the results of his bloodwork: to my astonishment his blood sugar level was at six grams! In my entire career, I had never seen such a figure. It was an unbelievably high rate. I immediately called Moncef in and had him hospitalized that very evening in the diabetes department. His pains were related to a diabetic neuropathy.[3] I analyzed his entire medical report. What was most incredible was that all the previous glucose levels had been strictly normal. Moncef was treated with insulin for a few months, and his diabetes was stabilized. He was better from a medical point of view, and, more importantly, his psychological condition also improved. Once again, he was sleeping properly. And now—and I have no idea why—for the past two months, the situation has been very dire. One day, during a consultation, he confided to me that he was desperate. He no longer had any faith. He even thought that everything that had befallen him was due to a *shour* sent by his first wife. That is why I wanted us all to meet today."

The *Shour*

Even before our session, Moncef had confided to the referring hospital physician that he was the victim of a *shour*. In other words, he was the victim of a sorcery attack. Making a statement such as this in a medical consultation room is quite exceptional. It is testimony to the confidence that the patient placed in his physician. And it is also likely that because Dr. Margot-Duclot had already attended sessions of transcultural mediation and had an interest in anthropology that these words, usually confined to the private sphere, could be spoken out loud.

The concept of a *shour* to explain phenomena is so widespread in the Maghreb that it is almost a banality (Claisse-Dauchy, 2000). The *shour* refers both to a concept, the sorcery attack, and an object, whose production involves the principles of destruction used in sorcery to strike the victim. The object may be made from diverse elements: nail clippings, hair from the head or body of the targeted person, their writings, excrement, and so on. The object is then hidden, often along a path taken by the intended victim: the threshold of a house, the bathroom, or under the bed.

Once the object has been discovered, an initiated healer, in Tunisia known as the *talib* or *fquih*, is called in to neutralize it. Sometimes, the healer may identify the attacker and turn their attack against them. Our experience has shown that patients may bring us the *shour* object they have found to demonstrate the reality of the attack. Recently, an Algerian patient told us that after the sudden death of his young brother in a car accident, he found the *shour* shut in a bottle that was hidden in the tree in the garden of his late brother's family house. Moncef was convinced that his medical condition was the consequence of an attack arranged by his first wife. According to him, she was trying to avenge herself of the serious damage caused by their conflict-ridden separation. And in fact, the *shuwwafa*, the fortune teller whom Moncef's family consulted, confirmed that the origin of the attack lay with the woman. This interpretation was not sufficient for Moncef: it did not stimulate him to play an active role in his treatment and thus break out of his isolation. That day, a full year after his fall, his condition was still cause for great concern. He was suffering just as much, and periods of sadness alternated with periods of anger. His married life was becoming a nightmare. Every day, he was overwhelmed with a feeling of helplessness, convinced he was of no use to society. Dr. Margot-Duclot had suggested on numerous occasions that he meet with a psychiatrist, but he would not hear of it.

Although the theory of a *shour* as a possible cause was under discussion, at this stage of our encounter, we believed it was too soon to go down that particular path. We suggested that we should first examine the medical narrative in its entirety, with the help of Dr. Margot-Duclot.

Serge B. said, "We need to understand more fully how the physicians explain the sudden appearance of diabetes."

Dr. Margot-Duclot responded, "Stress may be the reason for the onset of diabetes, but there must certainly also be a genetic predisposition."

Moncef blurted out his conviction, "I think I caught it because of the surgery. I trusted my surgeon, but I was very frightened all the same. I am still terrified when I remember waking up. I was told I was unlucky because I came round too soon. I was still in the operating theater"—he shivered—"and I thought I was dead and in hell. In hell, they say there's fire, but around me there was only blood." He hesitated, searching for the right words. "How can I put it?"

Leila O. came to his help. "In Tunisia, to express what Moncef felt, the *khal'a* would be mentioned."

Moncef agreed, "Yes, that's it!"

Leila O. continued, "In our country, this word is far stronger than 'fear.' It's a form of aggression that is feared terribly because it is both unpredictable and inexorable."

"That's exactly how I felt the situation to be."

Serge B. explained to Dr. Margot-Duclot, "It's as if the *khal'a* has broken into the envelope surrounding the subject, allowing disorder to set it. It may be an illness, a jinn,[4] or an *aïn*, known as the evil eye."

Dr. Margot-Duclot seemed surprised and turned to Leila O., "So, you too think that a trauma can trigger a medical condition such as diabetes?"

Leila O. responded with a polite smile.

Two theories of disorder intersect when it comes to the interpretation of a trauma. The theory of the physician refers to the stress; that of the mediator refers to the *khal'a*. These two theories are based on a specific conception of the person, their nature, their links to the world, and consequently the disorders likely to affect them. Behind an apparently similar facade, the routes taken by Western medicine to explain the sudden onset of diabetes and those of the explanatory Tunisian model are completely disparate—hence Leila O.'s polite smile.

Dr. Margot-Duclot said, "For the past few months, Moncef has been very sad. It's as though his will to live, his vital spark, have been extinguished."

Leila O. turned to the patient, who sat up straight to listen to her. "With all due respect to Moncef, I think it could be said that his *nefs* has been affected, and his strength as both a man and head of a family has been undermined." The group looked at her enquiringly, and Leila O. continued, "In the Maghreb, it is said that each person is comprised of two principles: the *nefs*, linked to the emotions, and the *rūḥ*, which can be translated as 'breath' tied to the will. The *nefs* is transmitted to us by our mother, and the *rūḥ* comes to us from God."

Serge B. asked, "So, if we want to help Moncef, do we have to treat both his body and his *nefs*? What do you think of that, Moncef?"

Moncef thought, hesitating before he responded, "I feel that the problem has deep roots. I have no strength left; no motivation for anything."

Dr. Margot-Duclot resumed, "Since these problems began, he often thinks of his mother. He's spoken to me of her often during our consultations."

Catherine L. asked Moncef, "Does she help you with your problems?"

Moncef looked defeated and answered, "She's dead."

"I'm sorry to hear that. Did she die recently?"

Moncef said very sadly, "Over twenty years ago."

Moncef's emotion was so strong that we might have thought that his mother had died recently. His deep depression was obvious, and he was so intensely upset that we could better understand the background to his story.

Catherine L. spoke, "When one's life force is so deeply affected, it is natural to turn to one's mother. Does she visit you in your dreams?"

Moncef was still very emotional and answered, "No longer, not since the surgery. Because despite the medication I take, sleep is still very difficult for me. I sometimes spend hours tossing and turning in bed. Then, suddenly, I will fall into a heavy sleep. But I no longer dream."

We asked the patient to tell us what medication he was taking. He gave us a long list of his pills: antidepressants with analgesic properties, hypnotics, painkillers—all medications hardly conducive to nighttime dreams.

Serge B. addressed the group: "I wonder who in his family Moncef can turn to for support. Perhaps to his father?"

Moncef said scathingly, "It's as if I no longer have a father!"

Serge B. asked him to explain.

Reluctantly, Moncef said, "He hurt my mother; he hurt my brothers. He abandoned them. . . . He was the first to arrive in France, then he brought us over—my mother, my older brother, my two sisters, and myself. I was ten years old at the time. For the three years when we all lived under the same roof, the household was filled with screaming and arguments. We finally learned that he had taken another wife when he arrived in France and had children with her. If my mother had not returned to Tunisia, she would not have survived such a betrayal. After that, my older brother stayed with my father, and I returned to Tunisia with my mother and my younger sisters. I was the one who took care of them. Can you imagine? I was thirteen years old! Since then, I've always managed on my own and never counted on anyone else."

His words barely masked the strength of his resentment. Yet, he told us that he always treated his father with respect during his sporadic visits to the village. Each time they met, Moncef hoped that his father would give him a gift, however small. "And I'm still waiting for one," he said, smiling sadly.

This disruption in Moncef's life gave us some insight into the root of his fragility. To his own surprise, he was expressing it for the first time, in the context of a hospital meeting. Now he said,

"I've been sick for months, and not once has he called me, even though he knows how bad my condition is."

Serge B. turned to Dr. Margot-Duclot, saying, "These are all painful memories. Moncef is profoundly hurt. He is still very angry with his father. I wonder if he'll be able to get over this anger. Yet, perhaps one day, he will have to."

Dr. Margot-Duclot asked, "But why? He's clearly explained that he wants no further contact with his father."

Serge B. said, "Let me try to explain. Earlier, we said that at the time of the surgery, there was a 'breaking in' of what we can call Moncef's psychic envelope. Since then, he has become fragile. In Tunisia, this would be expressed differently. It would be said that he is no longer protected and thus anything can affect him adversely, both diabetes and the *shour*."

Dr. Margot-Duclot responded, "I think I understand what you mean. You are worried about Moncef because, unless I'm mistaken, in the Maghreb, protection is guaranteed by the paternal lineage."

Serge B. agreed, "You're right, Anne. In a patrilineal system, I only exist because I am the son of my father, and he links me to all our common ancestors. In this context, we understand some of Moncef's problem. Because belonging to this lineage was something he found intolerable, he is cut off from all forms of family protection."

Moncef leaned heavily on his crutch. We had been talking for close on two hours. Too many emotions had surfaced; too many painful memories had been raised. We suggested that we end our session and meet again soon, if Moncef was willing. But before we all took leave of one another, we asked his physician if his treatment could be reduced somewhat so that he could participate more actively the next time, and, mainly, so that he could start dreaming again.

One Month Later

We were back in the same consultation room. Moncef still had his crutch, but as soon as the session began, he placed it near the coat hangers. He seemed to be better, and his face was more relaxed. More importantly, he was very much present with us; his spirit seemed to have been freed.

Leila O. summarized the conversations she had had with him and his wife, and then the conversation turned again to the death of Moncef's mother.

Moncef told us, "When my mother died, it was really terrible. It's true, and I admit it, that I was traumatized by this story." His tone became almost aggressive. "And today, who else thinks of her? Every time I return to Tunisia, I go to her grave. I clean it and keep it in good condition. But I'm not her only child. I have brothers and sisters who should take care of it. But they do nothing."

Serge B. addressed the whole group. "In his family, it's as though he bears everyone's responsibility. Can we express it like this?"

Moncef seized on Serge B.'s suggestion. "It's me, rather, who carries the parasol for the others." He thought a while. "So that the sun doesn't burn my brothers and sisters."

Serge B. said, "That's exactly it, it's to protect them. But who carries the parasol for you, Moncef? Until she died, your mother did. And today, who's taken over the task?"

Catherine L. now said, "His father should do it. But Moncef holds such a bitter grudge against him that this old story seems to have paralyzed the entire situation."

Now Leila O. spoke up, "That's the crux of the matter. For us, a father is always a father, whatever he does. Moncef, despite everything he's been through, has a son's obligations to his father. But in exchange, his father must protect his children and grandchildren." She turned to Moncef. "Isn't that the way things are supposed to be?"

Moncef, decidedly disturbed, answered, "That's true. That's how it should be." He looked for a tissue in his pocket and mopped his forehead. Then the troubled moment passed, and he once again joined in the discussion actively. "During the first mediation session, you said that my treatment should be adjusted so that I could dream. Well, recently, I had a dream. I was very upset because I hadn't had any dreams for months." Seemingly amused at what he was about to say, he continued, "It was a rather strange dream. It's hard for me to relate it to you. I dreamed about computers. You know, computers have a 'brain.' I dreamed that I was searching for the brain that controlled *all* computers."

Serge B. asked, "Can you explain in more detail what you saw in your dream?"

"I saw the computer. It was like a ball, with strings hanging on either side."

"If I understand correctly, you were not searching for this computer but for the brain that controlled all computers. Is that it?"

"Yes, that's right."

"Ah, now that's a surprising dream. What do you think, Catherine?"

Catherine L. said, "I'm concerned about Moncef's worries. He has serious worries. He wonders about the meaning of things, the meaning of life itself. I think he's asking a fundamental question: Is there someone who's coordinating all of this? Or is each one of us a small computer, isolated and unconnected?"

Moncef answered, "The one who coordinates is God."

Serge B. said, "But you are wondering where God is to be found."

"You have to work to find Him. . . ."

Very quickly, Moncef made a connection with an old memory of a figure in his family, an exceptional person. "You know, I had an uncle who was a saint. When he arrived somewhere at night, people would say that he was surrounded by light. He had unbelievable powers!"

Catherine L. asked, "Was he an uncle on your father's side?"

"Yes, he was the brother of my paternal grandfather. One day, I had a serious problem—a throat infection that made it very hard for me to breathe. My mother took me to consult him. I was only a child, but I remember it as clearly as if it were yesterday. I was overawed by this uncle, a man respected by all. He looked at me intensely and then took out a sugar cube and spat on it. He wiped the sugar over my neck. Then, he ordered me to eat it. This event is not something I was merely told about; I experienced it myself! And believe it or not, a few hours after I left, I was cured."

Dr. Margot-Duclot did not hide her astonishment.

Leila O. said to the group, "I'm not at all surprised by what Moncef has told us. In Tunisia, some people have very strong healing powers. This power is never individual, but it belongs to the family and, beyond that, to the entire community. These are gifts that can be found over several generations. When these healers die, they may become saints, and their graves are sacred sites of pilgrimage. There are some very famous saints, reputed for what they can heal: it may be skin affections, the infertility of a couple, behavioral problems, and all manner of other issues. It's a well-known belief system, and even today it is still very strong. Everyone knows these places, which are frequently visited. It's something like Lourdes here in France."

Catherine L. went on, "In fact, this power lies within the paternal family. Those are the closest family members. But Moncef has been cut off from them for years, since he stopped seeing his father. The question we must ask is how he can get his hands on this family strength and access the protection of his father, even though he's still angry with him."

Moncef was now sitting up very straight in his chair as he awaited our suggestions.

Protection

During our first session, Moncef had suggested that the *shour* lay at the root of his misfortunes. But we were not convinced that this was why the patient had remained entrapped between somatic illness and depression for so many years.

During our second encounter, using associations of the ideas and the dream that he related to us, we suggested a second interpretation to him. It did not mean the first was excluded; rather, our suggestion came into play at an earlier stage—that of the failed family protection.

Protection is a wide, flexible concept that can make sense both in the medical world of the West and in that of the patient. If someone's organism cannot rely on its own defenses, be they biological, immune, or psychological, medical science readily accepts the idea that they are vulnerable to disease. In the Maghreb world, it is believed that an individual who is deprived of fundamental forms of protection becomes a prey—the target of the negative influences surrounding them. Attacks perpetrated by a *shour*, an *aïn*, or a jinn, the invisible beings that owned the world before the appearance of humans, are often fearfully mentioned there, and belief in them is still very much present in migrant communities as well.

In a system of patrilineal relationships, the fundamental protection of a person is bestowed by virtue of their belonging to the paternal lineage. The ancestors transmit their *baraka*, their blessing, upon the person. But in order to receive the blessing, the person must regularly pay homage to the ancestors during pilgrimages to the founding place of the lineage, making sacrifices to the memory of the departed, and giving *sadaka*, sacred charitable offerings to the poorest. In this system, protection is activated not for the individual alone but rather for the entire group for whom he is responsible: wife, children, and all the direct descendants. The healing gift of Moncef's great-uncle is a gift shared by the entire family. We interpreted it as potentially usable to protect the patient. But to access this power, Moncef would have to go through the living representative of the paternal lineage, the head of the family—his very own father. Despite the serious dispute between the two men, we would work with Moncef to enable him to regain his position in the traditional system so that he could at last have access to what was rightfully his: the *baraka* of his great-uncle.

Moncef had probably understood from our first session what was implicit in our approach. The dream he related to us and the link he made to the powers that existed in his paternal lineage, evoked during our second session, bore out his understanding.

Without Moncef's help, we could not have made any progress down this route. He guided us toward this new interpretation whose outcome would subsequently validate its efficacy, or not. Moncef agreed to follow this route with renewed energy because, at that precise moment, our recommendation was the right one for him.

For our third encounter, Fatima accompanied Moncef. She told us that for a long time, she felt that the rupture between her husband and father-in-law was harmful to their family. When Moncef explained the conclusions that we'd reached during our first two sessions, they confirmed her intuitions. She would be the one to take the message to her father-in-law. She divulged to us that she had organized the family's forthcoming vacation to Tunisia so that they could accomplish the required rituals. She described her plan in detail, telling us how son and father could finally meet. She intended to deploy, she said, all the finesse and subtlety that women use in such circumstances. The objective was clear: it was necessary to obtain her father-in-law's permission to hold the commemorative and protective rituals in the *zaouïa*, the religious building where the great-uncle lay at rest.

Before she left us, Fatima turned at the doorway to thank us at length for giving her back the husband she knew before his illness. As Moncef warmly shook his physician's hand, he said to her, "Dr. Margot, I would never have believed that we could talk of all these matters at the hospital! Thank you once again. I'll keep you posted as soon as I return from Tunisia."

Seven Years Later

The phone rang several times before a young voice answered. It was Ahmed, Moncef's eldest son, who politely handed the receiver to his father.

Serge B. said, "Hello, Moncef. This is Dr. Bouznah speaking."

"Ah, hello, Dr. Bouznah. How are you? It's good to speak to you again after all this time."

Seven years had passed since our last encounter, and Moncef greeted me as if we had not lost touch. I was contacting him because, together with the rest of my team from the Centre Babel, a non-profit organization that carries out transcultural mediation in Paris, I was organizing a symposium at Paris City Hall about cooperation between physicians and patients faced with chronic disease. I wanted to present the testimonies of certain patients from our transcultural mediation sessions. Moncef was the first on my list of patients to contact, and he agreed immediately to my request.

Through Dr. Margot-Duclot, I knew that Moncef's health had improved. Most importantly, his pains had completely disappeared, and he had stopped the antidepressants several years previously. But I had no idea of the impact our sessions had on his life trajectory.

On a rainy morning in November 2017, we all met again—me, Dr. Margot-Duclot, Leila Oudrhiri, and Moncef—in the same consultation room, recently renovated, at the Fondation Rothschild. Catherine L. had other obligations that day and could not join us.

Moncef had not changed much, beyond perhaps having gained a little weight. Most importantly, he walked with ease, using his crutch more for reassurance than support. He was smiling and visibly very happy to see us again. We had filmed a video during our first encounters in 2010. That day, we were going to watch the sequences I had selected as being the most significant.

Our conversation picked up as though we had seen each other the day before, erasing the time that had elapsed.

Dr. Margot-Duclot opened the discussion: "When I met Moncef, his attending physician told me that he was very depressed. He was taking antidepressants and anxiolytics. But Moncef was aware that he had to make changes in his life; he also knew that he didn't have the solutions to do so. And it's true that we physicians readily make out prescriptions when we see a person suffering. We think we're going to give some happiness pills, but they don't always work. . . ." She turned to Moncef and said, "And when I asked you to tell us what you say in your culture when something as serious as an illness strikes, that's when you spoke to me about the *shour*."

I then suggested we screen the video we shot in 2010, when we had our first encounters. The sequence we showed to Moncef had the effect of a psychoanalytic interpretation and awakened associations and new elaborations.

We discussed the origin of the sorcery attack and the meaning of Moncef's dream, and then we went on to screen the key sequence that dealt with the forces that had to be activated in the paternal lineage, as well as the need to renew contact with his father.

Moncef seemed profoundly affected by this scene and began speaking. "You helped me open up to talk about this. Why? Heaven knows, I couldn't talk, at least not about matters like that. We keep them for ourselves for our entire lives."

Then, Leila O. said, "I remember very clearly when you said to me that you would never go to see your father, for you believed it was up to him to call you."

Serge B. said, "Yet, Moncef was brave enough to take the first step. Perhaps we helped him by giving him the strength to do so."

Moncef agreed, "Yes, in fact, I saw my father again the summer following the mediation sessions. And you know what? It was just like way back when. We spoke heart to heart. Then, three years ago, my father fell ill, and I went back to take care of him. I accompanied him through the last five months before he died. In the morning, I would go and see him. I'd come and go because I had to keep an eye on the building work of the house I was having constructed. He would wait for me to arrive and would worry when he didn't see me."

We felt Moncef's restrained sorrow. After some moments of silence, he continued, "Because you opened my eyes." Serge B. responded, "I think we only opened a door for you: *you* went through it. It's important to enable people to change . . ."

Moncef continued Serge B.'s phrase: ". . . to see things differently, to think differently. How fortunate that you were there because otherwise I don't know where I'd be today. Perhaps in my grave."

The revelation moved us all profoundly. Never would we have imagined the extent to which Moncef's life was shaken. And to think that he found the strength to confront his old demons to take his place by the side of the father he criticized so fiercely!

Let us leave it to Moncef to close this chapter: "I don't know what it is that you possess." He hesitated. "A heart, a liver, or maybe even a brain that makes it possible for me to talk to you without hiding anything. I still don't understand how you do it. I'd never spoken to anyone about my father or my mother. But I kept wondering who this Serge was, thinking he was a human being just like me."

5

When the Black Cat Bit

January 2003

Center for Pain Assessment and Treatment, Fondation Adolphe de Rothschild, Paris

In attendance: Alhassane T., the patient; Dr. R., the referring pain treatment specialist; Stéphanie Diakité, transcultural mediator; Serge Bouznah and Félicia Dutray,[1] facilitators

First Encounter with Alhassane T.

He walked confidently into the consultation room, where we were already seated. He greeted everyone present affably and sat down, hesitating for just a few seconds as he found the most comfortable position. Nothing in the way he walked, besides a slight stiffness of his torso, could lead anyone to guess that he had an artificial left arm. A scar that emerged at the inside corner of his right eye to disappear into the corner of his lips formed a strip across his face, attenuating his wide smile with a somewhat tense expression. Dr. R., who headed the Center for Pain Assessment and Treatment, had told us little about Alhassane. We knew that he came from Guinea, that his native language was Susu, and that he spoke perfectly fluent French. Stéphanie D., the mediator, had filled us in with these details before the encounter began. We learned that the Susu are one of the many Mandé peoples, and that they populate the area along the Guinean coast, particularly in Conakry, the capital—they total nearly three quarters of the population. Traditionally, they have been farmers. The majority are Muslim, even though in ancient times they fought the Fulani (Peuls), who were fervent proselytes of Islam.

Dr. R. began by thanking Alhassane for being present, and then took the floor: "What I want to make clear today is that the reason for this mediation session is not directly tied to a problem of medical treatment. Alhassane was sent to me one year ago by a colleague, also a pain specialist, who treated him for neurological pain following the amputation of his left arm. In 1999, Alhassane was seriously injured in a car accident in Guinea. The trauma was so violent that he had to be amputated at the upper third of his humerus."

Serge B. asked, "Do you mean to say that his arm was completely crushed by the accident?" Alhassane answered before his physician could speak. "Yes, that's what happened."

Dr. R. continued, "His orbital floor was also fractured, and there was facial contusion. He underwent corrective surgery." Serge B. turned to Alhassane. "Is the scar on your face the one caused by the accident?"

Without a word, Alhassane took a student card from his wallet and handed it to us. The card was very old. It bore the photo of a student aged about twenty, smiling cheerfully at his future. It was very hard for us to recognize Alhassane, even if certain features had remained the same. After the accidents, several surgeries had considerably modified his face.

Dr. R. continued, "He also suffered thoracic trauma with multiple rib fractures and cranial trauma. He arrived in a coma and was immediately taken into the resuscitation unit."

Serge B. asked, "When you describe everything that he underwent—the cranial trauma, the crushed thorax, the coma— do you mean to say that he almost died?" Alhassane, once again stepping in before his physician could respond, said nonchalantly, his tone in striking contrast with the seriousness of the account, "But that day, I didn't have an appointment!" To which Serge B.

said, "It was not decreed. . . ." Immediately, Alhassane responded, "You're quite right. That's exactly what *we*[2] say."

Dr. R. continued, "Today, his pain is responding fairly well to treatment. But at our very first consultation, Alhassan told me about his sleep problems. He had frequent flashbacks of his accident and his wakening at the hospital."

Serge B. asked, "Does he remember only those two specific moments?"

"Well, if I understand correctly, it's a traumatic scene that he relives while asleep and that wakes him. During the day, when he's busy, he doesn't have such thoughts."

Alhassane agreed.

"Generally speaking, this type of phenomenon is frequent in the months following a serious trauma. What is unusual in Alhassane's case is that he has a very precise memory of what happened. Usually, after a coma, the person has amnesia that covers the trauma itself and sometimes even a period of up to two days preceding it."

In his physician's opinion, Alhassane was suffering from post-traumatic stress disorder. In this type of pathology, the appearance of the symptoms—recurrent nightmares in particular—follows a shock that occurred in a situation where the subject had a brush with death. Dr. R. had already suggested psychotherapy to Alhassane, but he refused persistently, believing that his problem did not fall within the scope of the discipline.

Serge B. turned to Alhassane, "Earlier, when your physician mentioned that you were hit by a car, you said, 'No, it wasn't a car.' What was it that hit you?"

Alhassane, dramatically, mimed the scene. "The *thing* hit me. I suddenly blanked out and I found myself under the car." He explained. "That day, I was driving the car myself. I was leaving the city, so I couldn't have been driving very fast—no more than twenty to twenty-five miles per hour."[3]

"If I understand correctly, you were in a car. Afterwards, you don't know exactly what happened, but there you were, underneath another car."

Alhassane said insistently, "No, under my own car. I had been in my car with two of my cousins. One was in the passenger seat, and the other one was behind."

"Were they injured?"

Firmly, Alhassane, said, "No, nothing happened to them. Nothing."

"Did they explain to you later on exactly what had happened?"

Alhassane thought for a long while, then said, surprised at himself, "To tell the truth, I didn't even ask them."

Serge B. was taken aback. "Now, that's really odd! You mean to say that no one told you how the accident happened?"

We found Alhassane rather disconcerting. In such dramatic circumstances, any victim would wonder how such an accident had happened. But he seemed far removed from any such questioning, as if the physical conditions of the shock that took him to the brink of death were merely of secondary importance.

Serge B. tried again. "But later on, did you ask your cousins any questions?"

Alhassane responded, "I never really had the opportunity because I was immediately rushed to the hospital, and then my arm was amputated. Actually, two surgeries were carried out on my arm in succession. One month later, I was brought to France."

Serge B. summed up, "So, you woke up from your coma, your life was no longer at risk, and you could leave for France for further treatment and to have a prosthetic arm fitted."

Alhassane, said, "Yes, for those reasons, and also to get away from the family." Seeing the astonishment of everyone present, he continued, "At night at the hospital, I had the impression that a black cat came to bite my arm." As he spoke, he used his hand to mime jaws closing on his arm. "And the arm was in fact amputated twice!"

Serge B. asked, "Now, about this cat. Did you feel it, or did you see it?"

"At night, it would come . . ."—he hesitated; it was obviously hard for him to find the right words—". . . in my dreams[4] . . . in the things that I see. I explained all this to my father, and he immediately took the necessary steps. He forbade all visits." Alhassane continued. "Then, my father went to see people to search . . ."—again, he seemed to be looking for the right word— ". . . to look for the evil spirits. For us, that's what the black cat symbolizes."

Dream, nightmare, night terrors—none of these terms can convey the experience that Alhassane lived through. A psychoanalyst would probably explain it through archaic fears or castration anxiety, and Alhassane would probably listen politely. But from his point of view, the black cat was real. He had seen it. What's more, he had felt its sharp teeth sink into his flesh. This vision was a warning message that his father immediately deciphered and which led him to organize all the means necessary to protect his son.

Serge B. asked Stéphanie D., the mediator, "Do you agree with the symbolism of the black cat, Stéphanie?"

"Yes," she responded.

"When we say 'evil spirit,' it's a translation.[5] In Susu, you must use another word, right?"

"We say *köué ra michi*, literally, 'the men of the night.'"

"When you mention men of the night, for me—I come from Tunisia—that immediately suggests matters of sorcery."

Alhassane reacted immediately. "Of course!"

Serge B. summarized for the group, saying, "If I understand correctly, after the accident, Alhassane was hovering between life and death. For a month, he was treated at the hospital in Conakry. When he awoke from his coma, he spoke of the black cat to his father, who immediately understood the dangers his son was exposed to and decided to send him to France as quickly as possible."

Alhassane added, "He sent me here for medical treatment of course, but mainly to protect me."

Hardly a few minutes had elapsed since the session had started, and already Alhassane had taken us to the core of an interpretation of sorcery. Yet, not once over the past two years of his consultations at the Pain Center had he brought up the subject with his physician.

Generally, patients do not confide such matters in us until much later on in the transcultural mediation, once a bond of trust has been established, when they feel they can share thoughts not usually expressed within the context of a hospital consultation. It is likely that the presence of Stéphanie D., the Susu mediator, acted as a gateway for Alhassane. She was not there to interpret because Alhassane spoke perfect French. The patient understood her presence as an invitation to speak of the Susu world. This is no doubt the reason why Alhassane gave us his interpretation of the accident in plain words. He no longer attempted to fit it into the logic of material causality—the car accident. For him and for his family, there was no doubt it was a sorcery attack.

The motive for such an attack may be jealousy, rivalry, or envy. A sorcery attack necessarily involves a tie between people, for it is impossible to attack anyone with whom one has no interpersonal relationship. The more serious the attack, the closer the sorcerer is likely to be to the victim (Dekens, 2007). That is why Alhassane's father immediately forbade all visitors to his son's ward and had him travel as far away as possible.

We think that Alhassane used the French term for evil spirits, *mauvais esprits*, to help us understand a highly complex Susu reality that he thought we interlocutors were unaware of. But in doing so, he circumvented the logic that would enable us to grasp the subtlety of Susu thought on sorcery. To unravel this fragile thread, it was essential that we avoid a hold-all expression that could encompass a wide, cosmopolitan range of invisible beings, from creatures in Haitian voodoo to the "Evil One" from whose power exorcist priests deliver the possessed. The Susu world has a precise definition of the system of sorcery, with a logic of attack and defense. Giving serious consideration to this interpretation, we would now seek to understand the origin of this attack and the motives behind it. To this end, we had to penetrate the logic of the family—in other words, identify the group behind the individual.

Serge B. took up the discussion, "I'm wondering about your father. Is he a man who has great responsibilities?"

Alhassane answered, "He's a very powerful businessman."

"So, he's a man with an important economic role as well as a political role."

"Definitely."

"Is he still alive?"

"Yes."

"Is he the head of the family? Or does he have an older brother?"

"He has an older brother."

Serge B then addressed the mediator. "Stéphanie, it's Alhassane's uncle who is the head of the family, right? Then, he's the one with the responsibility to protect the entire family group, I suppose."

She answered, "Yes, it's the oldest of the uncles who has this role of authority in the family."

Serge B. turned to Alhassane, who, for the past few moments, had been rubbing his chin pensively. "Do you agree?"

Alhassane looked uncomfortable. "Yes, well . . . he's the one with the authority, but there were a few minor problems with my father. And if I remember correctly, that's where it all started."

"Was there a conflict between them?"

"There was a conflict because, as I've told you, my father is an important businessman. He had a house built in the capital, and others in many other towns. But he still needed to build one in our home village. In our culture, if you have an important position, you absolutely have to build a house in the family village. And each time he sent money to his eldest brother for the house, nothing happened."

"Was your uncle using the money for something else?"

"That's correct."

Serge B., realizing what was at issue between the two brothers, reacted, "Oh, oh, that's bad."

Traditional Susu society has a high degree of hierarchical structure. At the top are the *horon*, the nobles and aristocracy, then there are the people of the various castes—blacksmiths, cobblers, and weavers—and lastly, the descendants of slaves. Filiation is patrilineal and the individual belongs to the paternal clan. Older men hold authority over all the members of the group. In this system, it is fundamental that the younger generations show respect to their elders, and younger siblings to their elder brothers. The open conflict between the oldest brother in the family, Alhassan's uncle, and his younger brother, Alhassane's father, took a potentially devastating toll. This conflict provided us with the matrix for the narrative that was unfolding before our eyes.

Alhassane continued, "Shortly before the accident, my father asked me to go and see the house in the village. He said, 'Go there during your vacation and make sure it's coming along.'"

Serge B. clarified, "In fact, he tasked you with building the house in the village."

Félicia D. interrupted, "More importantly, he was sending his son to keep an eye on the uncle!"

"That meant that, until then, the money your father sent had not been used . . ."

Alhassane finished the sentence, ". . . for the purpose for which it was sent!"

Dr. R. asked, "And all this happened prior to the accident?"

"Yes," answered Alhassane.

Serge B. suggested, "It was before the accident, and in my opinion, people probably said that that was one of the reasons for the accident."

Alhassane was immediately affected by Serge B.'s words. He had given us the interpretation of sorcery. Yet, this hypothesis, now reworded by Serge, seemed to touch a nerve. The man who until then had been putting up such a good show slumped a little in his chair. His sudden sadness was clear to all.

Serge B. addressed Dr. R., "Alhassane has been readily opening himself to us, but we can sense that at heart he is very sad, as if he has a burden weighing him down, and not only the burden of the accident. I really have the feeling that something is blocking his way."

Dr. R. said, "That's my feeling exactly. He had many projects. He was studying urban planning. He had just got married and he has a son. He had his whole life ahead of him. He was chosen by his father to take over from him. Is all of this called into question today?"

Serge B. said, "Alhassane and Stéphanie will tell us if they agree, but I think there is more than his position at stake here. People in Conakry must have said it was an attempt to eliminate him."

Alhassane suddenly sat upright. "Absolutely!"

Serge B. continued, "He was meant to die, but the attack failed. So, he *was* protected, at least enough for his life to be saved. But today, these forms of protection are inadequate because his life is on hold."

Félicia D. took up, "It's as if he was carrying things within himself that are not intended for him. I'm thinking of the conflict between the two brothers. We might suggest that the uncle could not allow himself to make a direct attack on his own brother, who probably had many forms of protection in any case. In this type of situation, the children become the default target."

Alhassane agreed. Félicia D. continued, "What we have to elucidate are the reasons for the conflict between the two brothers. Such a situation is not common among the Susu. In this matter, it seems that because Alhassane's father was so successful, he took a very important position in the family—perhaps so important that it challenged the traditional role of authority his elder brother held."

Stéphanie D. said, "In our society, the elders look out to see who is gifted enough to succeed and to pursue an education. The choice must have fallen on Alhassane's father."

Alhassane confirmed this, "He was the only one!"

Stéphanie D. continued her explanation. "Then, all the family members are expected to get involved, to club together so that the person succeeds in the name of the family. And when this person succeeds, they must give back in return."

Alhassane blurted out, "He *did* give back! It was my father who sent all the children of his brothers and sisters to school. There were at least twenty mouths to feed at home."

Stéphanie D. continued calmly, "His father fulfilled his duty, but the elder brother, who has the position of head of the family, was not satisfied."

Alhassane agreed, "Exactly."

Stéphanie D. said, "He was expecting more."

A long silence ensued.

Serge B. spoke to Alhassane, "And all this has impacted your life."

Alhassane spoke very bitterly, "There I was, living the life I loved, preparing for my final university exams, and suddenly everything fell apart."

Serge B. synthesized the information. "Do we all agree on the meaning of what has happened to Alhassane? There is rivalry between his father and his uncle. The wish of Alhassane's father to be in control of the construction of the house was an insult to the uncle. When he sent Alhassane to the village, he was sending a clear message to his elder brother: I don't trust you. It was a declaration of war! The problem was that he sent his son without protecting him sufficiently and let him tackle the situation alone."

Stéphanie D. said, "We have a proverb that says, 'You never see both ears of the donkey that is going to knock you over.' I think we could say that the father did not see the imminent danger."

Serge B. agreed, "You're right, Stéphanie. But it also means that he was distracted by other matters. He was taken up with running his business and could no longer see Susu logic, family logic. He was somewhere else, taken up with matters of power."

Alhassane interrupted vehemently, "Everything he was supposed to do, he did!"

"Excuse me, but there must be a missing link," said Serge. "Otherwise, you would not be in this impasse. You are blocked—blocked as if what led to the accident is still active."

"But how can we interpret the nightmares that upset him so much?" asked Dr. R. "When I spoke about them, Alhassane immediately brought up the subject of sorcery."

Serge B. said, "As far as I can see, his spirit is still caught up in the mechanisms of sorcery. They are still preoccupying him. They're paralyzing his life. *That's* what the black cat is!" A long silence ensued. "And until we identify exactly where we have to take action, Alhassane will remain stuck. Some think that in such circumstances, the cat—the sorcery object—must be destroyed. But wouldn't it be preferable to smooth over the old bitterness between the brothers and thereby appease their rancor, so that the person who sent the cat calls it back or destroys it? I would suggest that we try to get the families to reach out to each other, so that this long-enduring, open conflict may be calmed, and Alhassane can take his rightful place again."

In a situation such as this one, the *komotigui*[6] or the marabout who could be consulted by Alhassane's relatives would first suggest hunting out the sorcery object that would substantiate the attack and neutralize it. After that, the *komotigui* would suggest to the victim that they take retaliatory action against the person who had instigated the attack. According to Susu logic, the sorcery attack is an invitation to counterattack. This opens the path to endless score settling within a family. For Alhassane and all the other patients faced with this type of problem, we consciously avoid entering into the process of a vendetta, instead establishing new proposals to stop the attacks and counterattacks spiraling out of control. We seek to settle the conflicts at their very source, whether they be debts, transgressions, insults, and even conflicts regarding inheritance.

Alhassane was very still, deep in thought. "I've been amputated. I'm here in France. I do nothing; I no longer receive my adult disability allowance. I don't have a roof over my head. I don't work, and I've been sidelined because I'm handicapped."

Serge B. responded, "Your situation is intolerable. But I must emphasize that you're in an impasse, despite all your potential, because the matter has not been settled. That's what we think. You must find the strength to return to your rightful place within your family."

Since his accident, Alhassane, a warrior adrift in a covert fratricidal war, had been hiding from the wrath of his uncle. We had reached a crucial point in the mediation session. Would Alhassane accept our interpretation? We had gone along with Alhassane in the logic he used for the interpretation of sorcery, but our paths diverged when it came to explaining the dead end in which he was now mired. He believed he was safe in France, whatever he had to endure—he was living in deplorable conditions, far from his home country, his wife, and his son; he was stripped of his status as the eldest son. It was an exorbitantly high price to pay for a false sense of security, but he was prepared to pay it. The case we argued had shattered his certitudes. Not only was he not safe in France, cut off from those who would support him, but he was still the victim of a dispute worthy of a Greek tragedy. The pathetic life he was leading was proof. He had to act to defend himself. But what route should he take to regain his place as a man and his status as a father?

The first mediation session came to an end.

Five weeks later, a second encounter with Alhassane took place in the presence of his younger brother.

That day, Alhassane was accompanied by Karim, his younger brother, a slender man of about thirty. Looking slightly out of place, Karim sat beside his elder brother. He was elegantly dressed in a well-tailored shirt and jacket, tweed pants, and a green silk cravat. Alhassane was more simply dressed in a three-piece suit. The members of the professional healthcare team were all in attendance, except for Félicia D., unable to be with us. The relaxed atmosphere was in stark contrast with the seriousness of the conclusion reached at the first session.

Serge B. began, "How have you been keeping since our last meeting, Alhassane? "

Alhassane answered, "Okay, I'm moving forward a little. I've seen the social worker and an adviser at the employment agency. I've also dealt with some other administrative formalities. Things are progressing."

Dr. R. asked, "And the nightmares?"

Alhassane, almost nonchalantly, said, "You mean those things about the accident? Things are quieter on that front."

"Quieter?" repeated Serge B.

Alhassane smiled widely. "Yes, they've calmed down a little."

Dr. R. tried again. "A little or completely?"

"A little. What I see now are good things."

Serge B. turned toward Karim. "I'm very happy to have you here with us. We came a long way with your older brother during our first encounter. With his permission, I'd like to tell you how things stand now." Alhassane agreed without reserve. "We raised many questions about Alhassane's accident. We also talked about how outstandingly successful your father is. Your brother, too, was on the path to success. Speaking of which, Karim, what do you do?"

Karim answered softly, "I'm studying for an MA in political economics in Brussels."

"That must be a very interesting program," said Serge B. "What will you do after you graduate?"

"I've already been contacted by a large company. I'll be working in the field of economic development."

Serge B. turned to Alhassane, who did not hide his pride. "Your brother is a brilliant man." He turned back to Karim. "Your older brother was also on the path to success, wasn't he? He too should have graduated and made a successful career for himself in Guinea. But then there was that tragic accident. He was a young man, full of promise, married with a child. We had a long talk with your brother to attempt to figure out what the accident meant. Together, we examined your family stories. Your brother explained that in his opinion, it was not an accident. There was an attack behind it."

Karim confirmed clearly, "That's exactly what we all said. You know, in our country, things are different from here. There is polygamy. My father had several wives, and there were always conflicts and jealousy between them. My brother and I no longer have our mother to protect us. She died very young. I never even knew her." He stopped, very emotional, before continuing, "She was the old man's first wife, and everyone had their eyes on us. When the family members saw that we were doing well at school and that we were going to take our father's place, they turned against us."

Serge B. said, "The first to succeed was your father. Your brother explained that he was the only family member selected to go to school. The entire family invested in your father's success."

Karim seemed very surprised. "That's quite right."

"We could say that he was the hope of your family."

Karim smiled broadly. "But he's told you everything!"

The two brothers looked at each other, then burst out in infectious laughter.

After a few moments, Serge B. spoke again, "Are you surprised?"

Karim was still smiling. "You know, right now, I feel as though I'm back in my village. It's true, my father was the standard bearer of the family. There were ten brothers and sisters. He was the only one to go to school. You could say that the family centered on him; he was the focus of all attention. When people saw that we were ready to take over, we became a target to be knocked down, by any means at all." He turned to his brother, seemingly asking for his consent to continue talking. Alhassane concurred. "In our society, there are the natural forces and the invisible forces. Of course, they can't be explained scientifically, but they are there. Today, back home, people say that Alhassane is not even able to bring his wife and child over to join him. And no one is there to take his defense."

Stéphanie D. intervened, "For the moment, Alhassane cannot simply go back home. The question is: Who can represent him there in his absence?"

Karim responded, "The father, of course, could do it in such cases. But he can't get mixed up in this. It's not his role. It should be up to the mother."

Alhassane, who had not said anything until then, said firmly, "This is too trivial for our father. He can't possibly get involved in this."

To explain the patient's awkwardness, Stéphanie D. clarified his remark, "If their father intervened, he would risk triggering a conflict with his current wives and their children. He simply can't take sides with his two eldest sons openly."

Serge B. said, "Stéphanie, you're saying that there is fierce rivalry between the children. More exactly, strong rivalry between Alhassane and Karim, the children of his first wife, and the others."

Karim said firmly, "That's for sure!"

"And they're taking advantage of Alhassane's weakness and vulnerability to challenge the possibility of his taking the place as family head when he succeeds his father," said Serge B. "As a rule, all the brothers have to consult him concerning important decisions, isn't that correct?"

Alhassane spoke vehemently, "I even wonder if they didn't play a part in what happened to me. The issue was not only to challenge me but to eliminate me. Because, in fact, they can't *really* challenge me. I'm the oldest, and in Africa, no one can touch the eldest. They can't do anything against that. But somewhere, behind the scenes, they are pulling the strings."

Stéphanie D. said, "Yet, last time we met, Alhassane told us that everything had been done to protect him."

Alhassane agreed, "Of course!"

Serge B. concurred, "Yes, Alhassane is protected because he managed to save his life. But everything else—success, owning a house, having a job, having his family with him—has been put on hold."

Alhassane, for the first time, confirmed, "Yes, all that is on hold. Work, a home, my family life——that's the minimum I ask for. With all that, I'll recover my rank in society."

Serge B. said, "What I also understand is that Alhassane can't return home if he does not have this minimum. Without it, he can't take his rightful place there."

Alhassane responded seriously, "I'm not going to ask anything at all of any of my other brothers, only of Karim. I know that the others won't help me and that they'll say that I can't even buy a pack of cigarettes, or shoes for my wife, or even a shirt for my son."

"So, today, your word is worth nothing at all."

Alhassane sighed, "Nothing at all."

Serge B. stated, "Alhassane must not remain on his own to confront his problems. On the one hand, here in France, there are professionals in the relevant sectors who can help him with some of his issues. He has already contacted the social worker and someone at the employment office. This is very important, as he's taken the first steps to finding a job and housing." And then he asked, "On the other hand, what should be done back in Guinea for the situation to progress and to activate all the resources necessary?"

Very seriously, Alhassane, said, "So, I've made the necessary arrangements. I've contacted my father-in-law, who works here, in France. I explained the situation and everything we discussed here. He has gone back to Guinea." He turned to his brother. "When did he go back, again?"

"On the 5th."

"Yes, that's right. February 5. Now, he's ready and waiting for me. He's waiting for me so that we can do what has to be done. Because, you see, we have no mother to help us, and our father is not the one who's going to get involved in this business. So, if my father-in-law is willing to help, I'm happy to accept his assistance."

While Serge B. checked with Stéphanie D. that he had understood Alhassane correctly, Alhassane turned to his brother and ordered, "Give me that!"

From a black leather briefcase, Karim drew a large notebook and handed it to his brother. The first page was covered with tiny handwriting. Alhassane turned to Serge B. and his physician. "You see, doctors, I have to wash myself with sea water. I must sacrifice a red cock, a white cock, and an ash-colored ox."

Serge B. was surprised. "Did you consult someone for all that?"

Alhassane answered, "They sent me these instructions from home."

"So, someone consulted a healer on your behalf?"

"Yes. And they said, 'As soon as you come home, you must sacrifice these animals!'"

He handed the notebook to Serge B., who, together with Stéphanie, read the long list of what the healer prescribed. Serge B. said, "The amount of the sacrifice prescribed appears to bear out the seriousness of what is hanging over Alhassane. It seems that your father-in-law did things very conscientiously. Do you agree, Stéphanie?"

Stéphanie D. agreed, "He did it for Alhassane, as well as for his own family."

Serge B. asked, "But have you undertaken all these steps since our last conversation?"

"Yes," replied Alhassane firmly. "What's more, Karim's wife helped me a great deal. She has already gotten hold of the cocks. I have to tell you something: she's the younger sister of twins."

Realizing Serge's puzzlement, Alhassane explained in Susu what this meant. Stéphanie D. thought for a while, searching for the right words, then explained what this assertion implied, "She's a witch!" And she and the brothers all burst out laughing.

Alhassane explained indulgently, "That means that my sister-in-law knows things. She has powers."

Stéphanie D. continued, "She's not a witch in the sense of being destructive or working evil. If a child is born into a family after twins and then survives, it means that the child has powers."

Serge B., smiling broadly, said to Karim, "You live with a woman like that, do you?"

Karim looked delighted. "Indeed, I do."

"Good for you!"

Karim continued, "She's a university graduate. She practices law."

Dr. R. said, with a touch of humor, "So, she has two sets of knowledge."

"I'm very happy because I see that Alhassane has found allies and is no longer alone," said Serge B. "Having bonds and allies is perhaps the most important thing."

Alhassane added, smiling, "And *good* allies."

Serge B. nodded approvingly. "Goodness, you've made a lot of progress since our last meeting. What a long way you've come. You're working very fast."

"That's because you drew my attention to my problems," said Alhassane. "Before that, I neglected matters. Even the accident—and it's difficult for me as a Muslim to say this—was something I could have avoided because there were signs beforehand, warnings that I neglected. But now, I neglect nothing." He turned to his physician. "Not even my appointments with Dr. R. I'm always here for them!"

Serge B. summed up the situation. "You miss nothing now, neither your family and traditional commitments, nor your commitments here in France, for appointments for professional assistance."

"No," concurred Alhassane, "I don't want to miss anything again. It has cost me too much."

Alhassane had now emerged from the darkness. Three months later, he went back to Conakry to be reunited with his wife and four-year-old son. He followed the instructions of the healers his family had consulted to the letter. And thanks to the unwavering support he had obtained, he met with his uncle in their native village. There, he calmed the uncle's rancor by participating in a ritual of reconciliation. He once again took his rightful place as head of the large family. But the economic situation in Guinea was very tough, and so he decided to return to France to study computer science and find a stable job in the field. His wife and son would join him as soon as possible. He was now sleeping peacefully at night. The black cat never returned.

Since that blinding, Poseidon, the Earth-Shaker, though he will not kill him, keeps Odysseus far from his native land. Come, let all here plan how he might come home.
—Homer, *The Odyssey*, Book One

6

The Curse

June 2002

Functional Rehabilitation Unit of a hospital in the suburbs of Paris

In attendance: Jacinthe R., the patient; Dr. B., the hospital physician; Sahondra, the interpreter from the Interservice Migrants, a nonprofit organization; Catherine Lewertowski and Serge Bouznah

First Encounter with Jacinthe R.

"They won't give me back my daughter!" Barely had we taken our seats when Jacinthe's desperate cry surged from her inert body, strapped in by black leather orthoses[1] on her legs, hands, and forearms. She resembled a boxer ready for combat. Jacinthe had been confined to a wheelchair for nearly ten years. Had the situation not struck us so immediately as tragic, we might have been surprised by the appearance of this petite, nearly forty-year-old woman. We were meeting her for the first time that afternoon in June at the request of her physician. She was very pale, with a protruding forehead and rather bulging eyes that darted about constantly behind thick glasses. Her body was deformed by her handicaps, but her thoughts were racing; Jacinthe had no more time to waste. She had borne too many misfortunes, too much suffering, too much injustice. She fidgeted in her wheelchair, which was held in place by a large iron brake on the left wheel. Earlier that day, she had tried to end her life by throwing herself from the top of the staircase on the fourth floor of the shelter. She was already on the top step when one of her fellow residents stopped her.

"I told her that I had this appointment with you this afternoon. She persuaded me not to let myself go and told me to come to meet you. She found the right words and gave me a little strength to continue. But I'm so tired. . . ."

For weeks, Dr. B. had been worried about Jacinthe. Her physical and mental health had deteriorated sharply. Today, she wanted to send her back to the hospital without delay. But before, aware that there were elements of the situation that she could not comprehend, she suggested a session of transcultural mediation to Jacinthe.

Nineteen ninety: that tragic year was embedded forever in Jacinthe's memory. Yet, the year had started out on such a hopeful note. Jacinthe had arrived in France—albeit illegally—from Madagascar to continue her studies and pursue a specialization. She was pregnant for the first time but still unaware of it. During the third month of her pregnancy, she began to feel severe pains all around her back reaching down to her pelvis. The pains did not alarm her: they were episodic, and she was used to putting up with pain. But what did worry her was that it was becoming increasingly difficult to walk. A strange, uncontrollable pain would take her by surprise while she was out. She consulted a doctor—once, twice, ten times. Each time, she was told, "You're pregnant, and this is just a problem related to your pregnancy. Nothing to worry about." The reassuring words of the physicians did nothing to calm Jacinthe, who desperately attempted to find out what was happening to her.

Jacinthe said, "I knew perfectly well this was not normal. I knew because I had treated patients who had *that* in Madagascar."

Catherine L. asked, "You treated people?"

"Yes, in Madagascar, I was a doctor. I came to France with my husband to specialize in gynecology and obstetrics. But we didn't have our documents, and I couldn't register for the course I wanted. So, instead, I studied tropical medicine in Paris. I think I must have been infected while I was treating patients back in Madagascar.

The doctors here tried to reassure me, but I was pretty sure something wasn't right. First, I was hospitalized for a urinary infection that was resistant to antibiotics. I explained that I had problems walking and emphasized that the symptoms were getting worse. The resident who attended me regularly recorded that the neurological examination was normal. But I knew only too well that it wasn't."

Catherine L. asked, "What did you feel? What exactly was abnormal about the examination?"

Jacinthe responded, "When the resident asked me to walk, I would totter. But she disregarded that. No one tried to look any further. They all said, 'It's the pregnancy.' And in the meantime, the paralysis in my legs got a little worse every day. By the fifth month, I could no longer walk, and I was hospitalized again. I had difficulty urinating; I suffered day and night. But once the infection was treated, the physicians wanted to discharge me. I refused. I was outraged. I demanded to remain in the hospital."

Dr. B. confirmed the facts. The medical team at the hospital still shudder when they recall Jacinthe's stubborn fury.

Jacinthe continued, "A few days later, the residents carried out an intradermal tuberculin test on me. The reaction was immediate. Phlyctenular![2] Over thirty-five millimeters! I remember when the doctors did their rounds. They all looked at one another and left the room without a word. They remained in the corridor for quite a while, talking. When they returned, the head of the department told me I had to have a spinal MRI scan[3] urgently. My disease was already very advanced."

Dr. B. finished Jacinthe's account. "Jacinthe is right. For reasons I simply can't fathom, the diagnosis was made very late. Perhaps because she was an undocumented immigrant, she wasn't seen to in time. Perhaps also because in France we're no longer used to seeing this type of pathology. It's become extremely rare here."

Jacinthe said firmly, "Or perhaps also because my medical colleagues didn't really take me seriously. Can you imagine, all the examinations were normal! I think they believed for a long time that I was hysterical."

Jacinthe told us her story with barely any anger. Her clinical precision made the story so real that it seemed to be unfolding before our very eyes. While the medical professionals dithered, the pregnant woman's paralysis was worsening.

She continued, "The MRI scan revealed an abscess on the dorsal vertebrae. For the first time, they diagnosed spinal tuberculosis, also known as Pott's disease."[4]

Dr. B. confirmed, "The tuberculous abscess had compressed the spinal cord and had led to paraplegia. It was located in an unusually high position. Jacinthe was given TB treatment for eighteen months."

Jacinthe added, "Because my condition was worsening, I had a C-section when I was seven months pregnant. It was on February 21, 1991. My daughter was born premature and weighed only four and a half pounds."[5] Jacinthe stopped, overcome with emotion. "The baby was saved. I saw her only very briefly before I was transferred to a functional rehabilitation center in Boulogne-sur-Mer.[6] Just before I left, I asked the nurses to tell me about my delivery, to describe my baby, my Lily, to me. I was in such a bad way, so weak, almost unconscious. . . ."

Jacinthe cried for the first time, apologizing for not being able to hold back her tears. "I was in a pitiful condition, so thin you can't imagine, and completely paralyzed. When I got to Boulogne-sur-Mer, I asked for Lily not to join me immediately. I was too ashamed; I was desperate. When she was four months old, she was sent to a foster family not far from the rehab center. At the time, my husband and I were alone in France, and the rest of my family was in Madagascar. My husband did what he could, but he was soon overwhelmed. He was also undocumented, without a proper roof over his head. And he's a man and had no idea how to look after a baby. In the beginning, I'd see my daughter at the center for a few hours on Saturday afternoon, but I couldn't even hold her. Later, I would go by ambulance to the foster family on Wednesdays. That lasted for four years. Four years and four surgical procedures: arthrodeses[7] to consolidate the part of the spine damaged by the abscess."

Thanks to her treatment and to her determination, Jacinthe finally left the rehabilitation center. But meanwhile, she separated from her husband; as she put it delicately, she "gave him back his freedom." Handicapped forever, what life could she give the man she loved so much that she married him against the will of her family? Her youthful dreams had turned to dust.

Jacinthe gave us some of her family history. "My family is from the Highlands. We are Merina people;[8] I suppose you could say we are the bourgeoisie of Tana. My husband is from the north of Madagascar. He is a Sakalava[9] from a very humble background. I had to fight to be able to marry him. My family never agreed to this alliance, and my father has never said a single word to him."

Divorced and all on her own, Jacinthe went to stay in a women's shelter in Paris. Sadly, in a voice tinged with irony, she described her situation. "It's a shelter for single women. I've been living there for more than five years now. Look what I've come to—I who come from such a well-respected family. I managed to obtain custody of my daughter, but with no income or permanent roof over my head, I couldn't have her live with me."

Overcome by emotion, Jacinthe could not continue her story.

Dr. B. helped her by resuming the medical history. She explained the particularity of Jacinthe's paralysis as follows: "One of the complications of a lesion of the spinal cord is spasticity. That means extremely disabling contractures of the lower limbs; they curtail the patient's movement. When oral treatment is not enough, as in the case of Jacinthe, we insert a subcutaneous pump that administers a strong antispastic agent directly into the cerebrospinal fluid. With this treatment, she could now leave her bed and move around in a wheelchair. But in 1997, despite the pump, she had a severe episode of spasticity. To me, it was clear that she was suffering from exhaustion syndrome, both physical and mental. The state of stress she was suffering at the time most likely led to her medical treatment failing. This woman was facing so many problems on her own! The department psychiatrist diagnosed a major depressive syndrome and suggested intensive treatment. At first, Jacinthe went to her appointments but soon gave up, telling us that they weren't helping at all."

Since then, and despite increasingly powerful analgesics, Jacinthe's pain had not let up. She could no longer deal with the suffering and anxiety that overwhelmed her so often when she was alone in her room. But she continued to struggle, and her indomitable combativity paid off. She obtained her resident's papers, found a job in a research laboratory, and was finally assured that her application for handicap-accessible housing would be given priority. But what she wished for above all was to have Lily, by then almost a teenager, come and live with her. And that's when things got complicated.

Jacinthe took up her story. "When I wanted to take my daughter back, the foster family turned her against me. Every time she visited me, she said terrible things to me. . . . The family was threatening me. They wanted to keep my child. I informed the case workers of the child welfare services, as well as the social workers in both Paris and Boulogne-sur-Mer. I told everyone, but to no avail."

And then fate dealt her another blow.

"Then, my younger sister was killed in a car accident in Marseille." She lifted her thick glasses to wipe the tears flowing down her hollow cheeks. "It was during my exams; I was studying all the time. You see, I wanted to pass the exams in my specialty so that I could at last make my dreams of specializing come true. My brother-in-law was the first to call me. I was devastated. I couldn't believe it. Then, my older sister confirmed the awful news. Thérèse was dead. I asked the university for exemption from the exams so that I could travel for the raising of the body and settle all the paperwork for repatriation." A long silence ensued before she continued, filled with emotion. "I asked myself many questions about what had happened to us. We were a family of six brothers and sisters. I'm the second youngest. The problems had already started with my eldest brother, Harold, who lives in Tana. He's an alcoholic, and he is always threatening my parents to try to get money out of them. Then, my younger sister, Thérèse, died suddenly. Then, there's my other brother, Bernard, who lives in Rennes[10] and whose life has become hell because of headaches that nothing can relieve. Lastly, three months ago, it was my older sister, Raymonde, also involved in a serious car accident in Madagascar. Today, she's hemiplegic. Like me. That's when I said to myself. . . . I thought, at least, I believe. . . ."

Jacinthe hesitated. She was obviously very ill at ease. She sighed and looked at us questioningly, undecided. What else could she tell us? Her left knee suddenly itched; she rubbed it. Catherine L. asked her to go on. Jacinthe sat up straight, leaning as much as she could on the metal elbow rests of her wheelchair and murmured, barely audibly, "I thought there was a curse!"

A curse. The word fell like a bombshell.

Who knew Pott's disease better than Jacinthe. A physician and specialist in tropical diseases, she had experienced it personally and was still suffering the dire consequences more than ten years later. She knew the TB bacillus, the biological mechanisms of the infection, the clinical complications, the treatments, and their side effects, and yet, that summer's day, in consultation room number 7, she expressed her doubts openly: Was her disease not part of a larger chain of causality—that of a family curse? All delirium, any confused state could be ruled out, and her physician was there to bear it out. But Jacinthe proved that it is possible to understand the complex mechanisms of Pott's disease thoroughly and nevertheless associate the misfortunes that struck her and her family with forms of logic that were completely foreign to the world of Western medicine.

Over the years, Jacinthe had built up a trusting relationship with her physician. But this was the first time she had mentioned a curse. Dr. B. hid her surprise. She knew her patient—it would be more accurate to call Jacinthe her colleague—but she showed no annoyance that there were matters that Jacinthe had left unsaid. Having previous experience of transcultural mediation, she had learned that each patient constructs their own narrative to give meaning to their illness and suffering. She also knew that this narrative was generally not revealed within the framework of the usual sort of medical consultation. A different stage had to be set for such a revelation. Jacinthe, on the other hand, had divulged her secret thoughts because she realized that we were ready to hear them without denigration or judgment.

Jacinthe said, "I must tell you that the problems did not stop when my sister Thérèse died. When her husband recovered the money from her bank account, he sent it back to Madagascar to help my parents. Raymonde, my older sister, was as pigheaded as usual. She insisted on going to pick up the wire transfer when it reached a bank on the far end of the island, in Diego. Everyone in Tana knows only too well that the roads there are very dangerous. I had a sense of foreboding and tried to convince her not to go. I warned her, 'You're risking your neck!' But she took no notice. The day after her trip, her daughter told me that her mother had been involved in a serious accident. Today, she's paralyzed, like me, and it's because she wanted to collect Thérèse's money."

Sahondra, the transcultural mediator, shivered. Visibly upset, she said to us all, "In our culture, we don't touch the money of a dead person."

Jacinthe spoke to Sahondra, "And that's when I thought of a curse."

Sahondra turned to Catherine L. and Serge B. and said, "If you don't mind, I'd like to explain something to you. In Madagascar, the dead have a great deal of influence on the living. Of course, they're invisible, but they are an integral part of our daily lives."

The mention of Thérèse's death had awakened a fathomless sadness in Jacinthe. But little could we imagine exactly what was torturing her day and night.

Jacinthe gave more details, "When my little sister was killed in Marseille, the doctors phoned me to ask if I'd agree to an organ donation. I was in such a state of shock that I can't even remember what I answered. The next day, when my brother called me and said I'd done the right thing, I realized I'd given my agreement for the organs to be harvested." She cried. "In our culture, it is strictly forbidden to touch the body of a dead person. That's why I was so frightened of the anger of my deceased sister. When my brother had the body repatriated to Madagascar, I was in no fit state to travel with him. I gave him all sorts of advice, telling him, especially, to take rum with him. Because you don't just take a body back like that. You must trickle rum all the way, starting at the plane and right up to the cemetery. If not, there will be a problem on the way, for sure. When I heard that the trip went well, I thought, well, Thérèse agreed with me. She doesn't hold the organ donation against me. I was reassured, and at last I felt calmed. But now, with what's happened to Raymonde, I don't know any more."

Catherine L. turned to Sahondra. "In a story as dramatic as this one, Thérèse's anger might explain Raymonde's accident. But this hypothesis does not seem enough to us to explain *all* the misfortunes that have struck the family. Jacinthe has made it very clear that serious danger is hanging over all her brothers and sisters. In this situation, isn't it necessary to seek further explanations and go back on the family history? Sahondra, what do you think? What would be done in Tana in such a situation?"

Sahondra said, "I agree with you. I think that something very serious is weighing on the family. In a situation like this one, we would ask a Master, a man who knows how to decipher hidden matters. We go to see the *mpsiskidy*.[11] Have you, Jacinthe, and your family already consulted such a diviner?"

Jacinthe answered, "No, I haven't consulted a diviner. I went to church to pray. In our family, we've been Christian for several generations."

Sahondra continued her questioning, but spoke to Catherine L., "Fine, Jacinthe is Christian, but I'd like to know if her family respects Malagasy customs all the same. Being Christian doesn't prevent you from honoring your ancestors. In fact, it's very important in our country, even if half of the population claims to be Christian and the other half Muslim."

"No," said Jacinthe, "we don't follow those customs."

Sahondra seemed very surprised, but she was insistent. "But you went to the graves all the same? Did you take a little dust in a bottle? And the *razana*,[12] did you follow it completely?" She addressed the entire group. "Many people call Madagascar the island of the ancestors because we don't dare undertake anything unless we have the agreement and the blessing of our forefathers."

Dr. B. said, "I understand all of this, but Jacinthe left Madagascar over ten years ago. She's an intellectual. Her family no longer practices these customs. And perhaps she left all this behind a long time ago."

Sahondra responded, "With all due respect, Doctor, we never completely leave all these matters behind. They are part and parcel of us. We were brought up like that, in the spirit of the *razana*, which is the strength of our ancestors whom we must honor and respect. We have to follow the *fady*, the taboos and the rituals, to avoid angering them."

Jacinthe agreed with Sahondra's explanations. Even if she did not practice the customs of her country, she knew them, particularly the mortuary rituals that have to be carried out regularly so that the dead can live in peace in their world and protect the living. She told us that the following October, her younger sister's shroud would have to be changed during the *famadihana*. This time, would she be strong enough to make the trip?

The Turning of the Bones

Famadihana is a funeral custom practiced by most of the ethnic groups living in Madagascar (Sandron, 2011). The custom appeared relatively late in the island's history—some say during the seventeenth century—and is similar to the ancient custom of "secondary burial" widespread in Southeast Asia. The rite is based on the idea that the anima of the dead—the souls of the dead considered as divinities—only reach the world of the ancestors after a long period that may last for years, after the body has rotted completely and certain appropriate ceremonies carried out. The highly complex ritual is aimed at appeasing and venerating the dead. The time when the ritual takes place is also propitious for consulting the dead about important decisions concerning daily life. The ceremony begins with the exhumation of the body, which is then washed and wrapped in a new shroud. The family members parade in front of the newly covered body to kiss it, talk to it, sing it a song, or even dance with it. At the end, the ancestor returns to their last resting place, often with gifts. In Madagascar, this reburial, literally, the "turning of the bones," takes place every seven years during an important ceremony that brings together all the members of a group.

Serge B. turned to Catherine L. "For a while now, I've been wondering how Jacinthe's parents met. She told us that her family is from the Highlands. If we are talking about a family curse, we need to ask questions about the alliances involved—the alliance of her parents, of course, but perhaps also earlier alliances. We have to go back to the very roots to find the origin of any transgression."

Sahondra said, "You're right. As I was telling you, in our culture, a person does not exist alone. We were not born into individualist societies like in the West. Whoever we are, our name is tied to our clan both during our lifetimes and after death. That's why it's important to ask questions about names—the family name, of course, as well as the first names that are chosen."

At the mention of names, Jacinthe looked disturbed. She fidgeted again in her wheelchair. Hesitatingly, she said, "In fact, I've been wondering about my maternal great-grandmother for a long time. I carry her first name, Jacinthe, which I hate!"

At the very instant when she mentioned the name, her left foot, until then completely immobile, began to tremble, first lightly, but then it jerked violently, as if shaken by an invisible, uncontrollable force let loose for interminable seconds. Jacinthe was powerless to end the episode, and Dr. B jumped from her chair to help her stop the fury that seemed to have taken over her foot. It was several minutes before calm returned to the consultation room.

Dr. B. commented, "I think that was an episode of spasticity." Seemingly surprised, she added, "It was really very extreme!"

Sahondra sounded worried, "Unless it was the *tromba* spirits who were making themselves felt—the spirits of powerful ancestors."

Jacinthe did not react to the explanation of the mediator and continued her narrative as if gripped by an idea she did not want to give up. "I was told that my maternal great-grandmother owned slaves. We possessed land and wealth. It is said in my family that this woman was known to be a money grabber and to be extremely harsh, especially toward the slaves. I was also told that she sold the child of a slave to a colonizer who left for the island of Réunion. She was an infant, barely two years old, literally snatched from her mother's breast. Today, I sometimes think that we have to pay the price for that crime."

Jacinthe was busy putting together the scattered pieces of an enormous puzzle, lost between cities, villages, and oceans over several generations. The force of what she was discovering left her aghast. Ideas were buzzing around her head. She suspected impending dangers and understood what was implicit in our questions. She wanted to act—act now and waste no more time. Of course, she was thinking too of her daughter, Lily, her only reason to live.

"I want to go back as soon as possible, maybe even in July," said Jacinthe. "I feel that I simply must settle matters at home. She paused and then said, "But what will I do about my daughter?"

Catherine L. calmed her down. "There's no need to hurry. You should take your time. In this sort of matter, you know you can't act alone. The road is long and perhaps even fraught with danger. You need help and support. Your physician is here to calm your pain. But for family matters, all of you siblings need to gather your strength as one. You must come together, be united. As far as your daughter is concerned, the situation will be sorted out in good time because perhaps everything is linked." Then, she added, "We are all struck by the succession of misfortunes that has befallen your family. It's as if it's become impossible for all your brothers and sisters to found families and carry on the family lineage." Jacinthe nodded her agreement. "Do you think we can meet with your younger brother and explain all of this to him?"

Jacinthe said, "I think he'd agree because he's also starting to think that something's not quite right. He's been suspecting this since Harold, our oldest brother, who was studying mathematics in Moscow, had to return home suddenly because of a health issue—something that was most likely benign. In fact, Harold also went mad. He had fits of mystical delirium. He would stop people in the street and talk to them about God. I had him hospitalized in the care of a psychiatrist who was a colleague of mine."

Diseases, deaths, accidents—Jacinthe, her brothers, her sisters, and even their children were blocked on their life's journey. What meaning could be given to all these events? Jacinthe was convinced that she could no longer hesitate; she had to attempt to find answers. As she said herself, after having been stricken, could she be the one through whose actions the curse would stop? "Perhaps so," Sahondra ventured, "because she bore the first name of her ancestor—a formidable person whose legendary strength she had also inherited."

We had been talking for nearly two hours. Jacinthe was showing signs of fatigue. We could not resolve all the questions in one afternoon. Dr. B. agreed to postpone her patient's hospitalization until the next encounter, this time with both Jacinthe and her younger brother.

Two Weeks Later, Second Encounter

In attendance: Jacinthe and her youngest brother, Bernard; Dr. B; Catherine L. and Serge B. Sahondra, the mediator, was unable to attend this session.

Bernard, Jacinthe's youngest brother, had arrived that morning from Rennes, where he had been living for several years, studying sociology. His sister had already recounted to him the conclusions of our first encounter. She had also asked us to call him before we met to give him a clear explanation of the objective of this forthcoming session.

"Western medicine can help Jacinthe from a certain point of view. But for family matters, for what seems to be weighing over the children and even the grandchildren in your family, your sister needs you. If there are matters to clear up and protections to ensure, as Jacinthe wishes, two are better than one," Catherine L. said to him over the phone. Bernard instantly agreed to make the trip for the day.

This time, Jacinthe let her caring younger brother, who had decided to take the family destiny in hand, take over. With Jacinthe's agreement, Dr. B. gave a summary of her medical situation. Since our last encounter, Jacinthe's condition had improved. Her pains were less acute, especially at night, and the spastic episodes less frequent. Hospitalization no longer seemed to be a high priority.

Very quickly, the conversation flowed as if there had been no interruption. We discussed the funeral of Thérèse, their deceased younger sister, the harvesting of her organs, and the serious family conflicts triggered by the sharing of the inheritance. Bernard was able to fill in details and also confirmed the theory of a curse on the family.

Bernard said, "As far as the organ donation that has so haunted Jacinthe is concerned, we could say that our late sister agreed to it—she facilitated the entire process. If ever there was proof that she would have consented, that's it! Because, generally speaking, after a death there are any number of administrative problems. But in this case, everything went smoothly. Very quickly. Even the doctor said it was an amazing coincidence that one of my sister's kidneys was given to a sick child who lives in Rennes. That certainly gives me consolation. I know that in the place where I live, someone carries my sister's kidney. . . . Normally, I'm not superstitious, but I don't see how there could have been yet another car crash in the family. I immediately thought that a question of money was at the heart of the matter. Raymonde should never have tried to collect it. We never carried out the *famadihana* for Thérèse. So, perhaps she's calling for it. It's not easy these days because the ceremony is very expensive. But we no longer have the choice. After everything that's happened, we have to return to our sister's grave."

Catherine L. said to the group, "Bernard must be right. You have to pay tribute to Thérèse and honor her so that, in return, she gives you her protection. After that, you must elucidate what's happening in the family. You'll need to question the older generation and perhaps also those who can interpret secret matters. During our first session, Jacinthe mentioned that it was possible that there was an old story of revenge, or perhaps something more recent, caused by jealousy or disputes about money. But you might even have to look somewhere else, or farther away. . . ." She turned to Jacinthe and Bernard, saying, "We can be sure of one thing: you two will now be united in this quest."

Bernard said confidently, "Jacinthe and I have done a lot of thinking over these past few days. In our family, there are matters we have never really understood. For example, when we were children, we never went to our father's home to see his family.[13] In Madagascar, that is really unusual. I remember that my mother always used to take us with her to her family to 'drink a bowl of rice tea.'[14] Normally, the children, and especially the sons, belong to their father's lineage. They don't go to their mother's home, ever. The way things are, even when we die, we must be buried in the paternal family tomb." He paused to think. "I wonder why all our late family members are buried on my mother's side. Even our late sister, Thérèse. It was our mother herself who insisted that she be buried in her family grave."

Catherine L. suggested, "Children are a family's wealth. In your family, it's as if this wealth has been diverted by the maternal lineage."

What happened to cause such a profound break with custom that the paternal lineage was amputated? This question would be left open for the moment. It was now up to Jacinthe and Bernard to resolve the mystery. And to do that, they had to go back in time, engage with their family history, and bring to light buried secrets.

It was time to bring the session to a conclusion. The brother and sister were fully aware that they had to take action immediately. They decided to return to Madagascar soon, to pay tribute to their sister, and to consult a close cousin of their father's, a repository of the family history. They would provide support for each other through the long procedures that were to come—of that we were sure as we watched Bernard hug Jacinthe warmly and then bid us farewell before he wheeled his elder sister away down the long hospital corridor.

A few months later, Dr. B. gave us news of Jacinthe. When she returned from Madagascar, where she carried out all her sister's burial rites, she returned to work. Her pain had subsided, which meant that her medical consultations were less frequent. She met with the welfare workers, remaining calm throughout all the appointments. Although the daughter's return to her mother was not entirely settled, a meeting involving a mediator with the foster family was planned. Dr. B. never had her readmitted.

7

Leave Me Out of All This!

June 2018

Pediatric Nephrology Unit, Hôpital Necker, Paris

In attendance: Noella, the patient (also bears the name of Amy); the patient's grandmother; Dr. M., the pediatric nephrologist; the nursing auxiliary; the hospital psychologist; Fatou Dia, transcultural mediator; Serge Bouznah, the facilitator

A therapeutic alliance is essential in any case where the life of a child is at stake. Accompanying a family through such an ordeal to create such an alliance is a challenge that is even more complex when healthcare professionals and parents do not share the same cultural references.

Respect for people and their values, and the recognition of cultural particularities when faced with death are both fundamental to any ethical approach. How can we achieve this when migrants are involved and the healthcare team lacks any keys to decipher the behavior of patients and the families they encounter in often potentially tragic situations?

Meeting with Dr. M. in Her Office in the
Pediatric Nephrology Unit

Dr. M. opened the conversation. "I'd like to thank you for coming here to assist us. We are completely stymied by an adolescent we have here who barely talks. Noella is a young woman, fifteen years old. Her grandmother, a midwife, brought her here from Senegal for treatment. She has an HIV infection that has progressed to AIDS,[1] with very advanced renal insufficiency. She arrived in France in an advanced state of cachexia with disseminated BCGitis.[2] The treatment program is very intensive and means that the young woman has had to be completely uprooted from her home country for dialysis and, perhaps in the future, a kidney transplant. However, Noella has expressed her desire to return to Dakar several times. This jeopardizes our treatment program for her and challenges the route chosen for her by her grandmother. Noella seems to simply submit to all treatment and remains lying prostrate most of the time. We think that Noella's HIV infection is due to probable neonatal contamination—her mother died of AIDS in Senegal a year before the girl was brought to France."

Noella's Ward, at the Pediatric Nephrology Department, Hôpital Necker

Normally, transcultural mediation sessions take place in consultation rooms, but since the young woman was so weak, we decided to meet on her ward. Noella's grandmother, a very thin woman with an emaciated face hollowed out by fatigue, greeted us. Only a few scattered grey hairs gave away her age.

Noella was in bed, her head propped up by several pillows. Her hair was cut very short; her gaunt arms showed how thin she was. She watched us sit down around her bed. In addition to the physician treating Noella, the psychologist, the nurse, and the nursing auxiliary were present.

Fatou Dia, my transcultural mediator and colleague, originally from Senegal, was with us. All our conversations took place in French because both the grandmother and the young woman were perfectly fluent in the language. However, at certain times, when the traditional cultural approach to therapy came up, Wolof[3] was used.

During the session, which lasted nearly two hours, Noella, despite her evident tiredness, listened attentively to the narrative that concerned her. From time to time, she spoke up to clarify some of our questions.

The hospital physician, Dr. M., began. "I asked for this mediation session to be held because I am extremely concerned. We have to make important medical decisions that will impact Noella's future, but they involve complex treatment in France. And because Noella speaks very little, no one really knows if she agrees with our plans. We thought that this mediation session could help us make progress with Noella and her grandmother."

During the first part of the encounter, Serge posed questions to the physician and then rephrased the medical data in accessible language. The grandmother, with her knowledge of midwifery, followed our explanations without difficulty. This task of reformulating the medical background was mainly for Noella's benefit, and it seemed to capture her interest.

Very soon, we swung from the medical narrative to the story of her life. The grandmother told us that she had been unaware her daughter Hawa had AIDS until she died. In reaction to Serge's surprise, she explained, "You know, doctor, for us Fulani,[4] this is a taboo subject. Had I been aware of the diagnosis beforehand, I would have done everything possible to protect my granddaughter before she was born. But my daughter did not give birth in Senegal."

And she began telling the story, explaining the context in which Noella's parents met.

Until Hawa turned thirteen, when her father was killed in an accident—a terrible shock for the girl—she had lived a sheltered life within a well-off family in Dakar. When she was eighteen, she suddenly decided to leave the family home to see the world. Despite her mother's veto, Hawa emigrated to Spain, where she lived with distant relatives in Seville for a while. Very soon, she fell in love with her future husband—a Fulani man from Guinea, considerably older than she was.

Soon after their religious wedding, she got pregnant, but she said nothing to her mother until the baby was born. To make matters more convenient for the Spanish birth registration authorities, the child was named Noella. But the real name chosen by the father was Amy, after his paternal grandmother.

"And," said the physician, "Amy does not answer any of the staff when they call her Noella."

Raising questions about the issue of the patient's name enabled us, with the help of the transcultural mediator, to determine Amy's lineage membership. In the Fulani system, which is patrilineal, the fact that Amy's father chose to give her the name of his own grandmother provided her with legitimate alignment to her paternal lineage. Having established this, we could quickly tackle a narrative of which she was largely unaware.

Amy's parents separated very soon after her birth, thus putting an end to a period marred by violent quarreling. Hawa had learned that her husband already had a wife in Guinea. For Hawa, this was not acceptable. So, she returned to her family in Senegal when her daughter was a few months old. The grandmother brushed over the ensuing tension-filled period to focus on Amy's medical issues.

It all started when she was six, with an acute episode of malaria followed by neurological complications that plunged her into a coma lasting several days, leaving the entire family in complete disarray. Thanks to appropriate treatment, she finally awoke from her coma, but several months later, Amy developed what her grandmother called a "rheumatic flare-up" that once again confined her to bed.

That was when the conflict between Amy's mother and grandmother erupted. Hawa, who had met with a marabout who foretold that the child would die if blood tests were carried out, refused all recourse to Western medicine. Of course, this was unacceptable to the grandmother.

She wondered out loud, "Perhaps my daughter already knew about the AIDS and didn't want me to know. . . ."

With no regard whatsoever for her mother's objections, and in fact without even informing her, Hawa left to consult a Jola[5] healer in a village near Kolda in Casamance.[6] And there she stayed with Amy for two full years. In Casamance, the child's health improved, thereby convincing Hawa that she had made the right choice. However, all ties with her mother had been severed.

Serge B. turned to the grandmother. "I must say, I don't quite grasp your daughter's personality, nor do I understand why she turned to the marabouts in opposition to your wishes."

The grandmother replied, "I think she got it from her father. My husband was a Lebu[7] who was very much attached to his people's customs."

Fatou explained, "The Lebu form a community in Senegal. They come from the Cap-Vert peninsula, where they were already living when the first colonizers arrived. Traditionally, they're a fishing people, but there are also farmers among them. They profess to be Muslims, but many have retained their animist practices."[8]

Turning to the grandmother, she continued, "It can't have been easy for your family to accept your marriage."

"Yes, that's true," said the grandmother. "For us, Islam is very important, but I loved my husband, and my family gave in. He was a famous musician who performed throughout Senegal." She continued her story of Hawa. "Hawa was very close to her father. Whenever he could, he would take her with him to visit his family. And despite my misgivings, he would often take her to ritual ceremonies. I think she must have even attended some *ndepp*, rituals of possession that the Lebu hold. When Hawa's father died, she was barely Amy's age. I know she suffered badly."

Hawa was thus brought up between two opposing worldviews: the Lebu tradition on her father's side, and modernity, with acceptance of medical science, personified by her mother. The sudden death of her father and then the onset of her disease sent her fleeing from modernity.

In the light of this narrative, it was clear that Amy was not alone at the center of the conflict: its roots went back to the preceding generation. One of the consequences of these conflicts, said the mediator, could be an absence of protection of the children and of Amy in particular.

To travel to Kolda from Dakar was no mean undertaking. But Amy's grandmother, anxious about the health of her granddaughter, braved dangerous roads to reach the marabout's village, where she demanded, using threats, that he allow the two of them to leave. Utilizing the reputation of her family and her powers of persuasion, she prevailed on the dignitaries of the village. Amy and Hawa returned to Dakar, but the grandmother said sadly, "Whenever my daughter went away, she would always prefer to leave Amy with a healer in the Dakar suburbs than have me look after her." She continued, "Perhaps she wouldn't let me look after her child because she feared I would take her for medical exams while she was away and learn about the disease. What's more, Amy herself would refuse to see the doctor when I suggested it to her. She sided with her mother and wouldn't even let me touch her."

Trapped at the heart of a fierce conflict of allegiance, Amy had no choice but to choose sides—as her mother had done when she fully embraced traditional medicine. Soon after, Hawa's health declined. When her mother attempted to have her treated at the Fann University Hospital in Dakar, Hawa once again fled to the healer, this time leaving Amy behind.

Amy listened attentively to the account of this narrative. Despite her obvious fatigue, she intervened from time to time, notably when Serge B. spoke of what she must have felt when her mother left to see the healer.

Serge B. addressed Amy, "You must have wondered why your mother used to go away. You must have sensed that everyone else was worried. Even if no one said anything to you at the time, you must have known that important things were happening."

Serge B. turned to the grandmother and the healthcare team and said, "I think Amy was a prisoner of this conflict, caught between her mother, who said certain things to her about her health, and her grandmother, with her medical training. We should not forget that Amy lived for a long time in the marabout's village, and she absorbed the reasoning there. She was in the middle of all this. Perhaps it's still difficult for her today."

He turned back to Amy, "I certainly wouldn't have liked to be in your position, having to choose between your mother and your grandmother. Honestly, I'd have liked to tell them, 'Grandmother, Mom, come to an agreement and leave me out of all this.'"

The large smile that lit up Amy's face bore out his remarks and confirmed that the conversation could continue. This was one of the key moments of the mediation session and helped deepen our understanding of the tensions that surrounded the young woman.

It is empathy that is crucial in enabling a therapist to construct a narrative together with the patient. The issue is not to put oneself in another person's position to feel what they feel, but rather to reach an understanding of the patient's experience, together with the ability to communicate through words. For Carl Rogers (2018),[9] it is the sincere expression of empathy that has therapeutic efficacy. Such interpersonal skills may lead us to share the feelings of another person transiently and to help us find the words to express what they could not admit to themselves.

The grandmother picked up the story again. "Some time later, the healer called me and asked me to come and fetch Hawa quickly. I immediately understood that the situation was serious. When I arrived at the village, my daughter was in a pitiful state. She was in a hut with the other women. She could not stand up, her legs were badly swollen, and she was breathing with difficulty."

In Wolof, she said to Fatou, who translated for us, "Before we left, the marabout tied a necklace of braided fibers around Hawa's neck. He said it was extremely important not to take it off during the entire return trip. But just a few miles before we reached home, the necklace began to come apart. And it was Hawa who removed it in the end."

Fatou explained to us, "It was a special necklace made of a particular kind of bark and is typical of animist fetishes. The grandmother even wondered if it wasn't the necklace that was intended to keep her daughter alive."

The grandmother took up the story again. "Hawa was still lucid at the time. She wanted to go straight to the hospital, with no detours. But I had to go home to pick up some of her things before I could take her to the hospital."

Then, her voice cracked with emotion. "It was such a shock. No sooner had we crossed the threshold of our home than she lost consciousness. We lay her down and tried to resuscitate her, to no avail. . . . She died in my arms."

Fatou went to the grandmother to comfort her. It was an emotionally charged moment for us all and of course for Amy too. She finally let her tears flow. This was the first time that she had heard the story from her grandmother. The older woman took Amy into her arms and cried with her. We were all overwhelmed with emotion. Only after a drink of water were we able to continue.

Fatou then spoke of the separation of Amy's parents. Since their breakup, Amy had not seen her father. But, she explained, the Fulani are patrilineal. Since the children traditionally belong to the paternal family, that side must ensure their protection. Even if the couple is separated, the paternal family still has this obligation.

How could the protection to which Amy was entitled be reactivated? This was the question that would be the focus of much of the mediation session.

Amy's grandmother greatly appreciated the suggestions we were making. Our aim was to appease the conflicts centered on the young woman and, more importantly, to ensure that all the available forces—medical and those of the family—work in symbiosis for Amy's protection. Amy told us that her mother visited her in her dreams. This gave us a lead, and Fatou suggested that Hawa could provide protection even though she was no longer alive. Amy described her as smiling and dressed in white, but she could not remember the words she uttered. We suggested she write down her dreams as soon as she woke up and then recount them to the psychologist, who was with us that day.

Working in liaison with the psychologists of the units where we intervene is also a crucial aspect of our functioning. Although a mediation session is, by its very nature, limited in time, it is often necessary to go over what transpires during the encounters with the children participating. Our mediation session had to answer a twofold question. The first was explicit and emanated from the healthcare team; the second concerned Amy and her grandmother.

The healthcare team wondered if they were not going too far in persisting with the treatment that Amy seemed to reject. Two months later, Amy's physician, the person who had requested the session, was interviewed by a psychologist carrying out research on the impact of transcultural mediation on the therapeutic alliance (Lachal et al., 2019). This is the light she threw on the question:

"It was very important for me," she said, "because the mediation session showed that there could be coherence and complementarity between the traditional world of the family and what we were doing for Amy at the hospital. After the session, thanks to what we learned of her story, we managed to give new motivation to the team so that they found renewed energy to work with her. Until then, the situation was psychologically very difficult for us all to deal with."

The second matter was the domain of Amy and her grandmother: the meaning of the illness that struck the young woman and the sufferings her family was dealing with. This was not explicit from the outset, and we had to construct it patiently together with the two of them, examining several aspects. What was the cause of the conflict between Amy's mother and her grandmother? Why did her parents separate? How could she, powerless as she had been to save Hawa, talk of her mother's death without being paralyzed by guilt the way her grandmother was?

To respond to these questions, we had to mediate between sometimes-conflicting voices and construct a new narrative that would at last bring meaning to behavior that otherwise appeared incomprehensible. Did we achieve this undertaking? The hospital physician provided some partial answers, and this is what she said, "I think that Amy understood that everyone was going to do their utmost for her. For the first time, we saw her show real interest in the account of the story we were weaving in her presence. It did not last very long because she was exhausted, both by her disease and by her treatment, but she was very much with us. We got the impression that it was the first time she was hearing her entire story and that it was vital for her. Shortly after the session, the grandmother managed to contact Amy's father, who spoke to her on the phone. Although Amy never told us what was said, we all realized how important this event was for her."

Transcultural mediation, whatever its benefits, cannot prevent a disease from progressing. The grim reaper had already laid his hand on Amy's shoulder. Eight months after our encounter, we learned that Amy had died from multiple infectious complications. Her grandmother, with the help of Fatou the mediator, took her body back to Dakar. Today, she rests in the Muslim cemetery of Yoff, in a grave close to that of her mother.

8

A Defaced Skin

Cyril occupies a special place among all the patients we have met. Transcultural mediation as we have been practicing it since 1998 is aimed at healthcare workers experiencing difficulty treating a migrant patient suffering from a somatic pathology.

Cyril, a French patient who called on us directly for a consultation, did not correspond to any of the categories of patients we had been treating up until then. Had he not been so insistent on meeting us, we would probably never have agreed to see him.

Thanks to him, we came to the realization that it was reductive to limit our approach to migrant patients only; its benefits could be extended. Cyril showed us that we could widen our definition of the transcultural encounter to one where the specific identity of the professional system treating the patient takes precedence over their cultural identity. Whatever the origin of a patient, entering a hospital is never an easy experience, involving as it does an encounter with a world whose codes and language the patient knows nothing about. This means that mediation and interpretation are required for all patients, including those considered to be native to the country.

Whether we are migrants or not, we are all custodians of narratives that contribute to our identity and that leave an imprint on us. These narratives are, most of the time, directly accessible. But unbeknownst to us, they sometimes take root in transgenerational stories.

We were able to help Cyril integrate new meaning into his story. In exchange, he opened a path enabling us to take new directions in our therapeutic practices.

Cyril called us one December morning. He had found out about us from reading an article published in a psychology review where our work was outlined. He was very interested in our approach and wanted to see us as soon as possible. Since childhood, he had been suffering from a debilitating form of chronic eczema, and he thought we could help him. Greatly disappointed to learn that we never meet directly with patients without a referral from their physicians, who would attend our sessions, he did not admit defeat. Cyril said he would immediately speak to the hospital dermatologist in Paris who had been treating him for years. Soon after, the dermatologist contacted us. He agreed to his patient's request, although, knowing something of our work, he was surprised that we would see a nonmigrant patient. We answered his questions and agreed to meet three weeks later at his hospital office.

December 2001
Dermatology Unit, Hôpital Saint-Louis, Paris
In attendance: Cyril, the patient; his dermatologist; Catherine Lewertowski and Serge Bouznah

A cold snap had suddenly set in over Paris, and snow had been falling over the city for two days. Cyril's dermatologist, a greying man of about forty, welcomed us warmly. He impressed us with his forthright and goodhearted nature. We were chilled to the bone from the cold and happy to take the coffee he offered. On his desk, we spotted a professional journal open to an article entitled *Dermatology: A Systemic Approach*. Seeing our interest, he told us that he practiced psychodermatology[1]—a discipline that combines classic dermatological treatment with a psychosomatic approach specific to skin conditions. The reason for his interest in our activity was now perfectly clear.

We spent several minutes explaining how we work, describing the dynamics of the session and the way communication is managed during this group session—all new to this hospital practitioner. We then ushered in Cyril from the waiting room. A man in his thirties, energetic, medium height, wearing jeans and sneakers, strode in. Through his thin-lensed horn-rimmed glasses, we could make out a slight squint in his left eye. An untrained eye would not discern any traces on his skin besides a mild, diffused redness that indicated that it was fragile. A large, well-worn leather bag was slung over his shoulder. Hardly had he sat down than he hauled out a tape recorder that he casually placed on the coffee table; only then did he ask for our permission to record the encounter. We gave our consent, but not without expressing some surprise. Although we often record our sessions for research purposes—with the assent of the patients—this was the first time a patient was taking such an initiative.

Catherine L. opened the session by addressing Cyril. "We are very happy to meet with you today. You took an unusual route to get here, but you certainly know how to use your powers of persuasion."

Cyril spoke softly but determinedly, "I'd like to thank you sincerely for agreeing to see me. I've been suffering for a long time. But this year, it's all too much for me. My outbreaks occur so frequently that I have to be hospitalized regularly."

The dermatologist said, "Five times this year, each time for a hard-to-treat problem of cutaneous superinfection."

Cyril practically interrupted his physician. "In fact, I've suffered from this eczema for as long as I can remember. My mother told me it started when I was an infant. It disappeared when I was six years old but started again when I was nineteen. Today I'm almost thirty. My life is like hell. I have such terrible itching that it drives me crazy, and it often keeps me from sleeping. I also have awful nightmares. I'm very worried because the flare-ups are becoming more and more frequent. They often affect my back, as well as my shoulders, the creases of my elbows, and my hands. If I don't treat them, I land up with huge oozing patches that become superinfected. And that means I go straight to hospital. Only one thing can calm them, and that's topical corticosteroid creams. But

I'm dependent on them, and they don't solve the underlying problem. Five years ago, I started psychotherapy here at this hospital. I must tell you, I've tried many other options: hypnosis, osteopathy, acupuncture, special diets. I've even consulted a magnetizer. Nothing really works, or if it does work, the effect doesn't last. Sometimes, during my outbreaks, my face swells. And when I have edema, I can't even look at myself in a mirror. I feel as though I've become someone else."

Cyril had told his story, analyzed it, scrutinized it so often, had searched so hard for explanations, and intellectualized his ailment to such an extent that we wondered what means we could use to create a connection with him.

Catherine L. spoke, "Today, if I understand correctly, you've turned to us in sheer desperation." He nodded in agreement. "What you describe is a terrible ordeal. I don't know if we'll be able to help you. But we are all here today, together, to try to help you. If you don't mind, I'd like to hear your physician's opinion on your disease."

Reluctantly, Cyril broke off telling his story.

The dermatologist began his account. "Cyril was one of the first patients I treated when I started working here six years ago. He suffers from very severe atopic eczema, which is the dermatological indication of an allergic reaction of the body. In medical terms, this is a hypersensitivity: an excessive reaction of the immune system to normally harmless allergens such as dust mites, pollen, or animal hairs."

Catherine L. said, "It seems to me that this disease may run in the family. Is this correct?"

The dermatologist replied, "Yes, these allergies often have a hereditary component. Several members of the same family may be affected. Research is currently being undertaken to find genetic clues, but today the causes have not been clearly elucidated."

Catherine L. asked, "And in Cyril's case, are there other members of his family who are affected?"

"No one," answered the dermatologist, "with the exception of his paternal grandfather, who suffered from severe asthma."

Cyril added, "That's what my father told me because I never knew my grandfather. He died a year before I was born."

Catherine L. continued to address the dermatologist. "Cyril has told us that his eczema started when he was six months old, then disappeared when he was six years old, only to reappear when he was nineteen. Do we know what can trigger outbreaks or, conversely, make them go away?"

He answered, "No, we don't know exactly. Often the disease starts before the age of two. Some say that external factors, like diet or weather, are responsible, but psychological factors, like stress, must certainly play a very important part. . . ."

Cyril again interrupted his physician. "I feel as though my eczema is like the absence of my skin—the absence of a protection that makes me sensitive to lots of things, both psychologically and physiologically. I don't know why it started up again when I was nineteen, but I do know what made it go away when I was six."

"Oh, really?" said Catherine L. "Do tell us."

Cyril began relating his story. "I worked it through in therapy. Six—that was how old I was when my parents separated. Let me explain. I'm the youngest in my family. I have two sisters: one ten years and the other twelve years older than me. I was the last to be born, and I came into the world because only my mother desired a baby."

"That's a funny way of putting it!" exclaimed Catherine L.

"Not really," Cyril responded, "because she decided to have me against the wishes of my father. Their marriage was breaking down, and she was trying to save it. She succeeded because I was born, and my father stayed for six more years with her. In fact, I was just a weapon in their war, and my skin was their battleground. When my father left, the eczema disappeared, but I remained alone to deal with my mother's loneliness."

Without any particular display of emotion, Cyril recounted his story. How many times had already he offered it up to a therapist?

The dermatologist now spoke again. "According to psychosomatic theory, the event that triggers eczema is often linked to a loss. The loss may be a bereavement, a move, or a break-up.

This loss is related to an early traumatic separation—one that is often unconsciously forgotten. Our skin seems to have its own memory and its own language, tasked with transmitting the unspoken matters of our lives. For Cyril, it seems that his birth was from the outset part of a breakup, and an unacknowledged one at that."

Catherine L. said, "If I understand correctly, according to this theory, starting from his birth, Cyril was the weapon in the battle between his parents. Since he couldn't express his rebellion with words, he displayed it on his skin."

In unison, Cyril and the dermatologist, said, "Exactly."

"And the paradox in this story," said Catherine L., "is that the actual departure of his father made Cyril's eczema disappear, at least for a while."

The dermatologist continued, "You know, we're starting to understand the mechanisms of the interaction between the brain and the skin. We've known for a long time that they both have the same embryological origin. They derive from the same structure—one that is formed on the twenty-first day of the development of the embryo. Recent studies have revealed that information is constantly circulating between the two organs. If you're under stress, or feeling emotional, the nervous system will translate this information into biochemical language via neurotransmitters that then act on the skin in such a way that they can induce, or cure, a skin disease."

Cyril and his physician shared the same theory based on the primordial role of the unconscious in the expression of bodily manifestations (Vust, 2010). The discoveries of embryology backed up their position. In the field of psychosomatics inspired by psychoanalysis, somatization is the only emotional language possible for patients who cannot express their affects, articulate their conflicts, and externalize their fantasies. The work of finding words to express what is really going on that is undertaken with the psychodermatologist, together with medical treatment, aims at overcoming this shortcoming. But for Cyril, after years of therapy, the psychosomatic approach seemed unable to deliver any more results. In other, similar situations, the therapist and patient would no doubt have admitted failure and bade each other farewell. But here, by inviting us to join his consultation in an effort to understand and help Cyril, the specialist agreed to call his theory into question so that other interpretations could be explored.

Catherine L. asked Cyril, "This theory is very interesting, but how do you explain the fact that your eczema started again when you reached the age of nineteen?"

"That's something I haven't figured out."

Anticipating Cyril's resistance, Catherine L. asked, "Would you like us to explore this together? Before you met us, you read up about our work. So, you know that we need to go into your family history."

"If you want, we can. But my background is fairly traditional, and we won't get much out of it. Also, I've talked about it a lot elsewhere already." Catherine L. indicated that he should continue. "I come from the south of France. When I turned nineteen, I moved to Paris to start a career as an actor. I was young, full of energy, and I threw myself headlong into my work. I wanted to succeed so that I could prove to my family that I could manage without them, but this disease put a stop to all that. Overnight, the rashes came back. It was always the same thing: red patches, then rashes, then terrible itching, with the episode reaching its climax on the fourth day. I was hospitalized. All my plans were completely overturned. At first, I wanted to overcome my problems on my own. But in the end, after a few months, I found a psychotherapist, who I continued to see for several years. The most upsetting thing for me is that the episodes flare up unpredictably." A long silence ensued, and eventually Cyril, obviously uncomfortable, continued. "Paris also meant that I could live openly as a homosexual. You know, it's not easy living in a small town in the provinces. Everyone keeps an eye on everyone else. I'm very sensitive to the gaze of others, perhaps because it was something I felt very early on my skin. In Paris, at least, I'm invisible. But there was a heavy price to pay. AIDS[2] killed my closest friends. Who knows why; I always slipped through the net."

Serge B. asked, "When you say you 'slipped through the net,' do you mean that you never caught the disease?"

"Yes," responded Cyril.

Serge B. spoke to Catherine L. "In Paris, Cyril's eczema caught up with him, but he escaped AIDS. Earlier, he was telling us that he experienced his eczema like the absence of any protection. I was wondering what forces protected him against AIDS. Perhaps they are to be found in his family. . . ."

Cyril seemed to stop short, disconcerted by Serge B.'s remarks.

Catherine L. turned to Cyril, "You've told us about the conflict between your parents, but we still know very little about your family, where they come from, and their story. And when Serge mentioned family protection. . . ."

Cyril said brusquely, "I don't have anything to say about my family. Since I've been living in Paris, I've cut all ties with my mother. I hardly see my sisters. The lives they lead are very different from mine. And as for my father, well, we see each other very irregularly."

Catherine L. stuck to her guns. "Your family name reminds me of a village in the southwest of France. Does your father's family come from that area?"

Cyril smiled. "No, you've got it completely wrong. My mother and her family are from Provence, but my father was born in Paris to Polish Jewish parents."

Catherine L. was surprised. "But what about your family name?"

Cyril answered, "That's a long story. In fact, I bear the name that my grandparents adopted straight after the war—the name of the village[3] where their family was hidden during the war."

Catherine L. asked, "But what was their family name originally?"

"Abramovitch."

Serge B. blurted out, "The children of Abraham."

Cyril sighed. He seemed annoyed. For the moment, the direction the narrative he was helping us to weave escaped him. Did that explain his sudden lassitude? Or was he resisting having to relinquish the leading role in his story? As for Catherine and

Serge, they exchanged glances, silent agreement that they could tap into their intimate knowledge of the Jewish community. And so, it fell to them to take up the position of transcultural mediators in this session.

The tape recorder on the coffee table began blinking. It was time to change the cassette. Cyril asked us for a few minutes to get the recording going again, and this short break provided much-needed respite.

Then, Catherine L. resumed the discussion by asking, "Did your father tell you the story of your grandparents?"

Cyril said, "A little, a long time ago. My grandfather came from a humble background, but he was a very cultivated man. He spoke four languages fluently. My father told me that he had always dreamed of going to France, which he called 'the country of lights.' He left Poland in 1935, leaving his entire family behind. During his wanderings, he met my grandmother, who was also fleeing with her parents. Together, they crossed Czechoslovakia and Austria. They reached Switzerland, from where they crossed the border and made their way to Paris. It was in 1937. My father was born in Belleville[4] one year later. When the Germans invaded Paris, my grandparents went to the south with my father. A couple of farmers hid them on a farm near Villeneuve-sur-Lot.[5] They remained there for the entire duration of the war. No one denounced them—they were very lucky. After the war, they were the only surviving members of two large families. All those who'd remained in Poland had been killed. That's when my grandfather decided to change his family name. My father was six years old at the time. What affected him most deeply, for as far back as he could remember, was the feeling of fear that was always present in his family. He never knew why. Of course, later on, he understood."

Catherine L. asked Cyril, "And how did he live with this story?"

"I don't think it really was a problem for him. Well, that's what I think because to be honest, I didn't really talk to him about it. He studied law in Toulouse, where he met my mother. She was the eldest daughter of a pharmacist. They married very soon after meeting, perhaps too soon. . . ."

"Do you know if your father had his bar mitzvah?"

"His what?" asked Cyril.

She explained, "His Jewish communion, if you like."

Cyril answered, "I've no idea. I doubt it. He's not even circumcised. And what's more, he can't bear anything to do with religion. Jews, Christians, Muslims—he lumps everyone together. He thinks that religion is a way of befuddling people. My mother is Christian and very religious. She couldn't stand my father's opinions on religions, and they argued bitterly about the subject."

Catherine L. continued her questions. "You told us that your grandfather died a year before you were born. Do you have a middle name? Could it be your grandfather's name?"

"How do you know?" asked Cyril, obviously surprised.

Catherine L. explained, "In the Ashkenazi community, it's customary to name a child after a deceased relative. It's a sort of continuity between the dead and the living."

"Joseph, like my grandfather's name. It's a name I never use." Cyril looked a little irritated. "Frankly, I don't understand what all this has to do with my eczema."

Catherine L. said, "You may well have the impression that we're making wide detours that are taking us away from your concerns. Don't worry, we're not losing sight of your eczema and the reasons that led you to meet with us. Can we continue together?"

Cyril agreed, probably out of politeness.

Cyril's reticence in exploring new avenues and letting go of his certitudes was clear to us all. At this stage of the meeting, we suggested adopting a technique that uses indirect communication. This involves participants other than the patient discussing the patient's history in his or her presence, developing hypotheses about the case or condition while allowing the patient the option of participating if he or she so wishes. This technique, used extensively within the dynamics of a consultation, often triggers extremely productive associations of ideas with the patient. But would Cyril be able to step back sufficiently?

Catherine L. continued, "Serge, I'm wondering about Cyril's story. His grandfather Joseph died just before he was born. So, it was logical to honor the dead man by giving such a precious first name to the first boy born into the family. As far as any disease is concerned, only this grandfather had allergy issues. Cyril and his grandfather have a double bond: in relation to the Jewish culture, through a name, and medically, through a disease. What are your thoughts?"

Serge B. responded, "Well, for a while, since we brought up the events of the war and everything that happened to the Jewish community, I've been thinking too that Cyril is a survivor in two senses. First, as the descendent of a Holocaust survivor, and second, because he escaped AIDS—the disease that was wiping out his friends. The reason I'm dwelling on the paternal family is because, in Jewish tradition, protection is considered to be provided by the paternal lineage. And this matter of protection is exactly what's been guiding our discussion since we began talking, right?"

Vehemently, Cyril said, "But I'm not Jewish!"

Catherine L. asked, "Why?"

"Because my mother's not Jewish."

Catherine L. turned to Serge B. "Serge, I'm sure you have something to say on the subject."

Serge B. smiled broadly. "You're being provocative! You know that it's a delicate question, and there are several points of view about it." He turned to Cyril. "You're adopting the position of traditional rabbis, who consider that Judaism is transmitted through the mother, and that this is the way it's been since the Torah was given on Mount Sinai. But today, progressive Jewish movements, especially in English-speaking countries, recognize the principle of both patrilineal *and* matrilineal transmission of identity. In my personal opinion, Jewish identity is a complex matter that can't be reduced to a formal definition."

Cyril was lost. He rubbed his hands mechanically, looked questioningly to his physician for support, then turned to us, the facilitators.

"Okay, then," he finally said, "But what are you getting at?"

We had reached a crucial moment of the session when Cyril's convictions were faltering. On the couch of the psychoanalyst who he had been seeing for many years, he had acquired intimate knowledge of his psychic interiority. The analysis had helped him in his ordeals. But today, it was no longer enough. Cyril had run out of options. All his plans had come to a halt. Hospitalized regularly, he was seeking to understand what befell him. Until then, having gone through so much psychoanalysis, he was in full control of the interpretations of his psyche. We were now suggesting that he step back from his position as expert and take a new route with us to a destination unknown to him. This temporarily uncomfortable position would, however, open up vistas he could not have foreseen.

Catherine L. spoke, "I'm continuing to think about your grandfather and the fact that he changed his last name. I wonder how he felt when he made the change. He must certainly have been scared that things would start again. But perhaps he was also angry with all those who were responsible for exterminating his family—the Nazis, of course, but not only them."

Serge B. asked, "Do you think he was also angry with God?"

Catherine L. answered, "Yes, exactly. I think he felt this way because anger with the God who had abandoned his people was a feeling shared by many Jewish Holocaust survivors. Some opted to lose their memory, while others lost their faith or took refuge in Zionism or Communism."

Almost cynically, Cyril said, "And my father became French, republican, and secular."[6]

Serge B. said to Catherine L., "You know what? I'm thinking of the story of Job. If you don't mind, I'd like to tell the story the way my maternal grandfather in Tunisia used to tell it to me when I was a child." He asked the dermatologist, "Do you know it too?"

"Yes, I remember some of it," answered the dermatologist, "but it would be good if you refreshed my memory."

Serge B. commenced, "My grandfather would always begin his stories with 'Once upon a time.' So, let's start the story. Once upon a time, there was a highly respected man called Job. Everyone admired his faith in God. One day, Satan, the adversary, said to God, 'It is easy for a rich man in good health with a large family to show You respect. But take all this away from him and I promise You, he will renounce You!' God took up the challenge, saying, 'I'll give you My servant Job, on condition that you do not take his life.' Immediately, Satan struck the household of Job with a series of misfortunes. He destroyed his worldly goods, with his herds of cattle, his harvests, and his home. Then, he killed all the members of Job's family: first his wife, and then each of his ten children. Lastly, he inflicted Job, now utterly devastated, with a terrible skin disease—one so severe that the poor man scratched himself until he bled. Every day, his friends would try to convince him, 'Give up your pride and repent. If God has punished you thus, it must be because you have committed many sins. Come now, confess!' Job always gave the same response: 'My friends, I have not sinned. I have remained faithful to the word of the Lord. I am in His hands. Only He knows why He is punishing me. May His name be blessed.' After months of suffering, Job had still not renounced God. Satan had to admit defeat. Then, God rewarded Job for his faithfulness by returning to him all his goods and his family."

Cyril listened closely. Then, he said, with a hint of irony, "Do I understand this parable correctly by concluding that my eczema is the result of a divine curse?"

Catherine L. responded, "No, not exactly. We think, rather, that there is a strong bond between you and your paternal grandfather. The tie is still invisible, but it also gives you strength. You know, the Bible, like all sacred texts, is an endless source of reflection for anyone who takes the trouble to go beyond the strictly religious dimension of the text. And what's more, your learned grandfather must have known all these stories from the Bible by heart. Perhaps he even told them to your father when *he* was a child." Cyril seemed troubled. "In the world of Judaism," she continued, "one only exists within a lineage. A name is not given simply so that it sounds good. It is thought to structure the identity of the bearer. If you were to consult a *rav*, he might say that you wear your grandfather's disavowal of his faith on your skin. I know that's surprising for you, but your condition could be interpreted in this way."

Suddenly, Cyril seemed interested. "And what would he do, then?"

"I don't know, exactly," said Catherine L., "because I'm not a *rav* but a doctor. Perhaps he would tell you to wash in water from the Holy Land or with water from the Dead Sea. Perhaps he would also tell you to go to your grandfather's grave to honor his memory and reactivate his protection. Speaking of which, do you know where he is buried?"

"My grandparents are buried in the cemetery of Carpentras.[7] My father told me this, but I've never been there."

Serge B. intervened, "That's a very old cemetery, sadly all too well known to Jews in France. That's where, if I remember correctly, many tombs were terribly desecrated." He spoke to Cyril, continuing, "And I think that took place in 1990, in May, to be exact. I remember the event because at the time the journalists linked it to the date of the anniversary of Israel's independence."

Cyril said nothing. Suddenly, his face crumpled. He rose from his chair as if he were about to leave the room, then changed his mind and sat down again with the group. He was very pale. We didn't know what was happening to him. His physician, worried, went up to him for support. For a long while, Cyril remained silent. Then, he excused himself and asked if he could leave for a few minutes to smoke a cigarette. He stopped the tape recorder and stepped out.

A few minutes later, Cyril returned; he had pulled himself together and continued, "I'm so sorry, but I was literally flabbergasted when you said that the graves were desecrated in May 1990. I don't know if my grandfather's grave was one of them. I can't really connect all the dots. Everything is very muddled, but it's exactly when my eczema broke out again, and I was hospitalized. It was when I arrived in Paris, at the age of nineteen."

Until that moment, Cyril thought that he had to face his disease alone. According to his narrative, the reappearance of the eczema when he was nineteen and the desecration of the cemetery of Carpentras remained two separate, unrelated events. The extent of his turmoil was a sure indication to us of the importance of the connection he established during the session.

Earlier on, given Cyril's initial resistance, we might well have been dissuaded from continuing the discussion. We would have reached a conclusion with him based on his convictions and our inability to bring new meaning to his story. But before we got to that point, we made Cyril a new offer: he should trust us and agree to listen to our dialogue about him. This dialogue—indirect communication—enabled us, via rich associations of ideas, to reach that very special moment of awareness, a true insight, at a crucial moment of the session, and that meant that Cyril now had to reinterpret his story completely. None of us could have anticipated his reaction. What we did know was that as we journeyed together, we gave ourselves the means to assemble the elements of Cyril's life and to weave together a totally new story using a perspective that was different from what had hitherto been offered to him—medical or psychoanalytic approaches. Without the system of the transcultural mediation session and the way we staged it, these causal links, which he could not have imagined, would perhaps never have emerged.

Cyril contacted his father, Maurice, very soon after our encounter. He asked if his grandfather's grave had been desecrated. His father was shaken by this unexpected call but reassured his son: although the tombstone had been defaced by Nazi tags, they had been erased. Cyril told his father about our transcultural mediation session, recounting the questions we had raised together. He asked him, as we had suggested, to accompany him to the next encounter. It took place six weeks later. Maurice came up from Toulouse.

During this second session, Cyril deferred to his father. He listened as Maurice recounted at length—most likely for the first time—the story of his childhood. Then, the memory of grandfather Joseph came up. Maurice told us that for years, he had been wanting to undertake a project that his father had entrusted to him shortly before he passed away: to see to it that the farming couple who, during the war, had risked their lives to save the entire family was honored with the title of "Righteous Among the Nations."[8] Maurice sadly acknowledged that he had never been able to undertake the procedure—one he felt obligated to do in memory of his father. When our encounter came to an end and Cyril announced that he wanted to visit his grandparents' graves, Maurice burst into tears.

A few months later, Cyril contacted us to give us an update. He told us that he had put his father in contact with the French Committee for Yad Vashem, responsible for the recognition of the Righteous, and that the process was on track. Insofar as his health was concerned, he had had no flare-ups of eczema for several months and had decided, in agreement with his dermatologist, to see a naturopath he had met during one of his trips to the south of France for treatment. He also informed us that he was returning to Carcassonne, not far from his father's home, to live for a while.

> The deepest thing in man is the skin.
> —Paul Valéry, *Idée Fix*

Conclusion

Isolated Patients in a Foreign Land

The world of medicine is constantly evolving toward increasing specialization and complexity. It moves in step with constant scientific discoveries and increasingly sophisticated technology. Today, in France, medical knowledge is divided into forty-four specialized fields; a century ago, there were just a few. Of course, growing specialization is undoubtedly one of the conditions for the success of biomedicine. But the compartmentalization of all these disciplines does not come without risk for patients in contact with health teams, depositaries of ever more narrowly focused portions of knowledge of the issues for the treatment they require.

In cases of chronic disease, where the patient has to traverse complex routes and encounter numerous healthcare providers, the parceling up of treatment is an obstacle to a comprehensive approach that caters to an individual's needs. There is a growing divide between the world of experts and the daily reality of those who seek out their services. This certainly exists in the case of certain migrant patients whose lifestyle, behavior, and way of thinking are sometimes far removed from generally consensual attitudes and theories in the West (Napier et al., 2017). But the issue can affect all patients, however, and far more subtle is the divide that exists with native-born patients. Equally, the impasses we have described may affect any patient. Such situations are not restricted to migrants and raise the question of the accessibility and intelligibility of the medical system whenever they appear.

However, it is certainly thanks to these migrant patients and the questions they raise that the patient–doctor dyad has been opened up to the presence of a third party, throwing light on the complexity of the encounter between the patient—all patients, in fact, and Cyril's situation is a case in point—and the world of the healthcare providers. For all patients, whether native born or migrants, entering the health system is an encounter with otherness. We need only think of the medical lexicon doctors use to address patients, closer to a foreign tongue for all those without medical training (Monseau, 2009).

In the presence of such learned professionals, mediation is necessary not only from an ethical point of view, but also as a potential practical tool. Its relevance and efficacy transform the prescriptive into the collaborative. Mediation illustrates that the physician's knowledge is complementary to the patient's knowledge, acquired through the personal experience of illness; this complementarity is productive (Lachal et al., 2019).

Transcultural Mediation: A Militant Undertaking

Some of our patients, for whom the language barrier seemed to have been an obstacle in correctly understanding their treatment program, had previous experience with interpreters. But the services those professionals provided was not enough. Linguistic scholars remind us that the word is not sufficient; its cultural context is necessary (de Pury, 2005). It is the *context* that the mediator reveals and that the patient confirms. Whereas interpreters re-say and strive to translate word for word, transcultural mediators use the patient's native language to enable the patient to express their affects, private thoughts, and, above all, their worldview. And this is sometimes necessary even for those of our patients who speak perfect French.

The mediator is professionally trained and well versed in transcultural clinical approaches. Very often, mediators are trained clinical psychologists[1] from the same ethnic group as the patient and are perfectly bilingual. Unlike interpreters, whose aim is a flowing translation from one language to the other, the mediator is expected to identify the rough patches that show up during the translation, for it is our hypothesis that at those spots where the folds[2] form, two worlds collide. From beneath these folds, between the interpretive systems of the caregiver and those of the patient, misunderstandings that may hinder treatment spring up. All the techniques we use in our mediation sessions are aimed at identifying such misunderstandings. It's not our objective to erase them, but rather to reveal the full force of the patient's universe and, if necessary, all the ways in which it contradicts the world of Western medicine (Bouznah and de Pury, 2009). In this delicate task, the mediator serves as our guide. With the active help of the patient and their family members, the mediator seeks out whatever is "rough" in the discourse, helping us to analyze these rough spots and bringing them out of their clandestine existence into broad daylight.

> . . . because speaking about languages, publicly discussing the translation of the patient's and his family's statements ipso facto turns the patient into an expert, a necessary partner, an ally in an enterprise of exploration, knowledge and especially of acting on negativity. . . . Talking about languages can bring everyone to agree. (Nathan in de Pury, 2005, 11)

The adage goes that the fish only realizes that water is vital to it once it's out of the fishbowl. An African saying has it that "It's in France that we learn what Africa is." Human beings live in such osmosis with the world in which they are born that they do not always know how to describe it and are even less capable of imagining how difficult it can be to live outside of it. Mediators are first and foremost men and women who have gone through the experience of immigration; they left their native lands to discover other countries. Lacking familiar landmarks, they create new ones. And so, they are capable of describing both the water in the bowl and the air surrounding it.

From our clinical practice, we have learned that the identity and personal experience of professional mediators are extremely productive tools when put to good use. We all bear signs that reveal our origins on our faces, in our names, and these are signs that patients can decode and use. Such signs filter into the entire encounter, imbuing them with a special tone. We believe that it is preferable for the connections to be made explicit. Otherwise, they may be obstacles in creating such connections. That is why, when we begin each of the encounters with introductions, we take enough time to explain who we are and—if we consider it useful—where we come from. Mediators, who usually meet the family beforehand, may make an even lengthier introduction, explaining where they are from, which village, and which family. Introductions such as these, which may seem incongruous to Western ears, are the very basics of good manners to non-Westerners—the means of identifying the Other to determine if one can confide in them. Over the years, we have learned that there are codes of sociability that underlie social ties between people. The relationship of "joking cousins" in West Africa allows—sometimes obliges—certain ethnic groups to make fun of one another, or insult one another, with no offence taken. A family of marabouts will command the respect of a family in which there are no marabouts. And there may be ties of persisting conflict between two clans that have been historically opposed.

Before our mediation sessions, the mediator often starts with the name and birthplace of the family to decode all that is implicit and that may either facilitate or impede the encounter. Our stance is far removed from the neutrality advocated by certain theoreticians of the act of mediation (Guillaume-Hofnung, 2001). In our opinion, the relationship between doctor and patient is profoundly unequal. If we were to stay neutral vis-à-vis this specificity, we would risk reproducing the imbalance and leaving the voice of the patient unheard. To truly bring to light the words of the patient, we believe that the act of mediation is a form of activism.

Narrating to Heal: Patients, Players in Their Own Treatment

The mediator, a third party, necessarily intervenes through a narrative. To grasp the unexplored, potentially unstable point of view of the Other, we—mediator and facilitator—need to shift our perspective, temporarily at least, from our own worldviews.

Ricoeur's "capable human being" is one who can narrate and narrate himself (Ricoeur, 2005). But can a narration heal? Both myths and the writings of philosophers and clinicians give us guidance. Each night, Scheherazade, the heroine of *A Thousand and One Nights*, tells a tale to her husband, King Shahryar, leaving it uncompleted. But so gripping are her stories that not only does she cure him of his murderous, depressive state, she also escapes the fate he had planned for her. In a completely different vein, Michael White and David Epston, clinical psychologists, established Narrative Therapy in the 1980s with the aim of helping patients to take their lives back into their own hands through the therapeutic power of narration (White and Epston, 2009). "Beginning a narrative conversation with a person is like starting out on a voyage over routes that are not known beforehand" (Laplante, 2009, my translation).

Thanks to Rita Charon, who founded the discipline of narrative medicine in the United States, the story of the illness that the patient tells the physician is now a core part of medical practice.

> Unlike scientific knowledge or epidemiological knowledge . . . narrative knowledge enables one individual to understand particular events befalling another individual not as an instance of something that is universally true but as a singular and meaningful situation. (Charon, 2015)
>
> Using narrative knowledge enables a person [*sic*] understand the plight of another by participating in his or her story with complex skills of imagination, interpretation, and recognition. With such knowledge, we enter others' narrative worlds and accept them—at least provisionally—as true. (Charon, 2015)

In each unique situation, we have built a narrative that brings together the entire set of points of view. Our script begins with the illness—it is the focus of the plot unfolded by the physician. The patient listens attentively. Converging on the diabetes of one, the eczema of another, the discussion between the players takes form. When all the questions regarding the medical facts have been dealt with, we suggest that the patient and their family share their point of view with us. And generally, that's when the patient turns to the specialist and asks, "Can I talk about things that we say at home?"

By this stage, we have journeyed along the usual paths of the medical interview. Can we exit them? In the hospital setting, can we seriously mention interpretations of illness based on laymen's theories unknown to healthcare workers, such as sorcery, curses, or the evil eye? The medical experts must take a stance, for their response generates the dynamics of the session. No patients expect a healthcare provider to believe in their interpretive system. Rather, the physician is expected to endorse the particular route the patient wants to take. Once such a go-ahead is given, the patient takes center stage, often displacing the illness object to the background. Patients rid themselves of an identity produced by the pathology as if it were no more than an item of old clothing and take on another role. They are now the principal player in the narrative they are telling. To enable this change to take place at the hospital, we must perform a balancing act at each encounter—an act that involves underlining the limits of medical action without detracting from its credibility. Without a close-knit partnership with the healthcare providers built on mutual confidence, our undertaking would be impossible. Indeed, it would have no meaning. This condition denotes both the strength and the weakness of our methodology.

In everyday language, a "patient" is the person who is acted upon versus the person who acts. The patient is an individual awaiting or under medical care and treatment. Seen from this perspective, the terms "patient" and "agent" are antithetical. Moving from one role to another—a semantic transgression— implies that the doctor authorizes the patient to make the move. Also essential is the "informed consent" of the physician, allowing the patient to act in accordance with their own values.

Expression through words is the first stage in the patient's reappropriation of their story. But the action that ensues is just as important. "Talking and the awareness of problems must lead to action. If not, reflection is nothing but idle talk" (Le Bossé and Lavallée, 1993). In each of our cases, the appearance of a new narrative has led patients to take meaningful actions of protection for the sake of their health and that of their family members. These include paying a bridewealth, setting up means of protection for a child, taking up their rightful position within their family, and accompanying a father to the graves of grandparents. None of the actions carried out by our eight patients was detrimental to their medical treatment. In each case, the treatment program was resumed, sometimes even reduced because of the improvement in the medical condition that initiated our intercession.

We might have feared that by agreeing to recognize their limits, physicians would disqualify themselves in the eyes of the patient. Nothing could be further from the truth, for after each of our mediation sessions, the patient's trust in the team of healthcare providers was strengthened.

Once our encounters were over, the illness was no longer a meaningless event, be it for Christelle and her family, Djibril, Alice and Pierre, Moncef, Alhassane, Jacinthe, Cyril, or Amy. On the contrary, their illness now informed the very meaning of their existence and encouraged them to break out of their isolation and regain their sense of agency.

Specialists Who Let Down Their Guard

The physicians who have called on us for our help have always done so voluntarily. All have expertise acquired over long years of medical practice. But confronted with incomprehensible difficulties in specific cases, they agree to drop their defenses. They are willing to be critiqued in the presence of their patient and of outsiders. All agree that thanks to a "failure," new possibilities can open up.

These healthcare providers are not resigned to considering that the patient alone is to blame for the impasse reached. They do not cast doubt on the veracity of symptoms they can neither understand nor alleviate. They do not systematically send patients whose conditions are beyond their comprehension to the psychiatrist. In the end, they accept the idea that medicine cannot understand everything, that the art of curing has its limits, and that the very recognition of these limits opens up fascinating vistas yet to be explored.

Without these practitioners, and without their trust in us, we could never have worked in hospital settings and experimented with our system within the framework of a hospital consultation. Without them, we could never have witnessed the unexpected resources of the patients, nor could we have shown how all players might benefit from such transcultural mediation. This is true for the patients and, of course, their families and, equally, all the healthcare providers.

We extend our warm thanks to each and every one of them.

Notes

Prologue

1. The Bizerte Crisis of summer 1961 was a diplomatic and military conflict between France and Tunisia, independent since March 20, 1956. It hinged on the fate of the naval base of Bizerte that had remained in French hands. The Tunisians wanted the base to be returned, and diplomatic tensions that had bubbled up in May when France started work to extend the airbase of Bizerte culminated in military confrontation from July 19 to 22.

2. The *rav* is the spiritual guide and authority on Jewish law. Certain *rabbanim* also act in a healing capacity with members of the community and sometimes even extend this practice beyond the community.

3. According to Jewish tradition, the name is the central element in anyone's identity—an integral part of their being. Manipulating a name is tantamount to manipulating the person. In the case of serious disease, the *rav* can change a name by performing a highly codified ritual.

4. Aimé Césaire was responding to questions put by Maryse Condé in an interview published in *Lire* magazine (June 2004), 114–120 (in French).

Introduction

1. HIV: human immunodeficiency virus, a virus that damages the cells in the immune system and weakens the body's ability to fight everyday infections and disease.

2. Those relating to causation.

3. The cult of the dead at All Saints' Day is still actively practiced in certain regions in France, with families sharing a meal on the tombs of their dead.

4. Michel Foucault offers an explanation for why these practices continue. "Instead of seeing in these religious practices a present-day residue of archaic beliefs, shouldn't they be seen as the contemporary form of a political struggle against politically authoritarian medicine, the socialization of medicine, the medical control that presses mainly on the poor population?" (Foucault, 2019).

5. The term "ethnopsychiatry" was created by Georges Devereux to take into account the fact that all cultures have constructed their specific models of interpretation and treatment of disorders, with western psychiatry not holding the monopoly of either (Devereux, 1972).

6. According to the official World Health Organization definition, traditional medicine is the sum total of the knowledge, skills, and practices based on the theories, beliefs, and experiences indigenous to different cultures, whether explicable or not, used in the maintenance of health as well as in the prevention, diagnosis, improvement, or treatment of physical and mental illness. In industrialized countries, adaptations of traditional medicine are termed "complementary," "alternative," "nonconventional," or "parallel."

7. Hôpital Necker-Enfants Malades is part of the Assistance Publique de Paris hospital network. As a reference teaching hospital, it is often called upon to treat particularly serious, complex pathologies. It houses more than forty centers of expertise devoted to rare diseases and is an important player in clinical research.

8. To ensure the anonymity of all those mentioned, and for reasons of confidentiality, all names have been changed, as, sometimes, have places.

Chapter 1   The Title Deed of Grandfather Léon

1. An IV pole (i.e., intravenous pole) holds bags for administering medicine or fluids through the patient's veins.

2. Central venous catheter: a large-gauge intravenous system that is left for a long duration, usually in a neck vein.

3. A diagnosis suggested to explain Christelle's symptoms. The malrotation of the small intestine on the mesentery would indicate a malformation such as an abnormal position of this part of the digestive tract.
4. Cystic fibrosis is a genetic disease that affects the respiratory tract and the digestive system.
5. An exploratory laparatomy involved the surgical opening of the abdomen to see if any lesion could explain Christelle's symptoms.
6. A chronic inflammatory disease of the pancreas.
7. Eight kilograms.
8. Democratic Republic of Congo was a Belgian colony until its independence in 1960. A large part of the population speaks French, and in a country where more than 200 languages are spoken, French is the lingua franca, along with Lingala. Congolese people often have French names as well as traditional names.
9. The Swahili and the Bakongo are members of the large Bantu-speaking group. Lingala is a Bantu language used by more than eight million people in the northwestern part of the Democratic Republic of Congo and a large part of the Republic of the Congo.
10. A symptom indicative of a particular disease or condition.
11. For a full theory of the term "to eat" (manger), see de Pury (2005).
12. Mami Wata (also spelled Mamy Wata, Mami Watta, or Mama Wata) is a water divinity in the Voodoo cult, widely practiced in Western, Central, and Southern Africa, as well as in the African diaspora, the Caribbean, and some parts of North and South America.

Chapter 2   An Angry Man

1. Principal region of Malian emigration to France, Kayes is also a major administrative entity where Soninke, Khassonke, Mandinka (Malinke), Moor, and Fulani people co-exist.
2. The Khassonke stem from the intermingling of the Mandinka and the Fulani and are members of the Mandinka group. The Soninke, also known as the Sarakhole, belong to an ethnic group found in Mali mainly along the Senegalese border between Nara and Nioro in the Sahel, as well as in Senegal and Mauritania.

3. Spinal fibrosis occurs after substantial destruction of tissues or when an inflammation affects a location where the tissues do not regenerate.
4. *Mori*: traditional Muslim healer.

Chapter 3   If You're a Human Being, Change Your Skin Immediately!

1. The Bakongo are part of the large Bantu group. They inhabit the region in the north of Angola, the Republic of the Congo (Congo-Brazzaville), the western area of DRC, and part of Gabon.
2. Gametes are specialized cells that ensure sexual reproduction.
3. Approximately four kilograms and fifty-three centimeters.
4. The infants' appearance was very similar to that of the Nit Ku Bon child ancestor described by A. Zempléni for the Wolof and Lebu of Senegal (Zempléni, 1985).
5. Keratitis-Ichtyosis-Deafness or KID syndrome is a rare congenital disease transmitted in an autosomal-dominant pattern of transmission. The disease generally presents at birth with a generalized erythema (rash) and ichtyosiform lesions. It is linked to a mutation of the Gap Junction B2 (*GJB2*) gene.
6. Drawing of amniotic fluid for analysis to determine, inter alia, chromosomal abnormality.
7. Capital of DRC.

Chapter 4   Who Will Carry the Parasol for Me?

1. A herniated disk is a bulge in which the outer portion of the vertebral disk is torn, forcing the inner portion (nucleus) to herniate through the fibers.
2. Nearly fifteen kilograms.
3. A secondary complication of diabetes, involving the peripheral central nervous system and vegetative nervous system.
4. Supernatural creatures in Semitic traditions. They inhabit deserted places, water sources, cemeteries, and forests. They are generally invisible and can take on various forms. They are capable of entering into contact with the human race.

Chapter 5   When the Black Cat Bit

1. Psychiatrist and anthropologist.
2. We Muslims.
3. Thirty to forty kilometers per hour.
4. For more on the status of the nightmare, see Nathan (2013).
5. *Mauvais esprit*: in French, literally "evil spirit."
6. *Komotigui*: in animist tradition, a spiritual master.

Chapter 6   The Curse

1. Orthosis: an orthopedic device fitted to an affected body part designed to remedy a functional deficiency of the musculoskeletal system.
2. An intradermal tuberculin test detects a tubercular infection. A phlyctenular reaction is the sign that the tuberculin test is unequivocally positive, indicating that the person has an ongoing infection.
3. MRI: magnetic resonance imaging.
4. Named after the English surgeon, Percival Pott (1714–1788), who first described spinal tuberculosis.
5. 1.95 kilograms.
6. A town on the north coast of France.
7. Arthrodesis: surgical procedure to fuse an articulation in order to stabilize it; also known as joint fusion.
8. The Merina are a people who live in the northern part of central Madagascar around the region of Tananarive (Antananarivo), the capital of Madagascar, which is known as Tana for short.
9. The Sakalava, Antakarana, and Tsimihety are the three main ethnic groups in the north and west of the island of Madagascar.
10. The capital city of Brittany.
11. *Mpisikidy*: a practitioner of geomancy, a technique of divining using shapes drawn in the sand.
12. The word *razana* designates both the ancestors and the respect given to them. It is a complex system of prohibitions and funeral rites.
13. Visiting the home signifies belonging to the lineage.
14. Rice tea, called *ranavola*, is a very popular traditional drink.

Chapter 7   Leave Me Out of All This!

1. HIV: human immunodeficiency virus, a virus that damages the cells in the immune system and weakens the body's ability to fight everyday infections and disease. AIDS: acquired immune deficiency syndrome, a number of potentially life-threatening infections and illnesses that occur when the immune system has been severely damaged by HIV.

2. BCG infections are rare complications specific to vaccination by the bacille Calmette–Guérin (BCG). They often present in the form of benign local reaction. Serious disseminated forms may occur in the case of severe immune deficiency, as was the case for Noella.

3. The most widely spoken language in Senegal.

4. The Fulani, or Peuls, are a traditionally pastoral people who inhabit the entire region of West Africa and beyond the Sahel-Saharan belt, a total of some fifteen different countries.

5. The Jola comprise the majority ethnic group in Casamance.

6. Casamance is a natural region of Senegal located in the south along the Casamance River, with a long history. Casamance borders The Gambia to the north and Guinea-Bissau and Guinea to the south.

7. An ethnic group that lives on the Cap-Vert peninsula.

8. Animism is the belief that a spirit or living soul animates living creatures—objects as well as natural elements, such as stones or the wind, and in guardian spirits.

9. Carl Rogers was the psychologist who developed person-centered therapy. He devoted his entire career to exploring the process of change in individuals and defining the principles that facilitate a person's development.

Chapter 8   A Defaced Skin

1. This approach is now used in dermatology. The first consultations to be so named were started in France in 1974 by Dr. Pomey-Rey at the Hôpital Saint-Louis, Paris.

2. AIDS: acquired immune deficiency syndrome, a number of potentially life-threatening infections and illnesses that occur when the immune system has been severely damaged by human immunodeficiency virus.

3. A hilltop town in the Languedoc area.
4. A Paris neighborhood where many newly arrived immigrants settled.
5. In the southwestern French department of Lot-et-Garonne.
6. The word in French is *laïc*, which refers to the separation of religion and the state. The adjectives "*laic et républicain*" are often mentioned together.
7. A town in Provence.
8. An award granted by Israel's Holocaust memorial authority, Yad Vashem, to honor non-Jews who risked their lives to save Jews from the Holocaust.

Conclusion

1. We have also worked with transcultural mediators who are healthcare providers from migrant cultures.
2. Image borrowed from mathematician René Thom's *Théorie des Catastrophes* (1977).

References

Baszanger, Isabelle. 1995. *Douleur et médecine, la fin d'un oubli*. French edition. Paris: Le Seuil.

———. 1998. *Inventing Pain Medicine: From the Laboratory to the Clinic*. New Brunswick, N.J.: Rutgers University Press.

Bouznah, Serge, and Stéphanie Larchanché. 2015. "Transcultural Mediation in the Management of Cancer Patients in the Tropical Area." In *Tropical Hemato-Oncology*, edited by Jean-Pierre Droz, Bernard Carme, Pierre Couppié, Mathieu Nacher, and Catherine Thiéblemont, 55–64. Cham, Switzerland: Springer.

Bouznah, Serge, Catherine Lewertowski, and Anne Margot-Duclot. 2007. "Une nouvelle alliance contre la maladie ou Quand les jinnas viennent visiter les médecins." *Douleurs: Evaluation–Diagnostic–Traitement* 8, no. 1: 8–16.

Bouznah, Serge, and Sybille de Pury. 2009. "La traduction, un outil pour guérir." *Soins Psychiatrie* 30, no. 260: 34–40.

Canguilhem, Georges. 2013. *Le normal et le pathologique*. Quadrige. French edition. Paris: Presses Universitaires de France (PUF).

Césaire, Aimé. 2004. Interview. "La culture c'est tout ce que l'homme a inventé pour rendre le monde vivable et la mort affrontable" *Lire* (in French), 114–120.

Charon, Rita. 2008. *Narrative Medicine: Honoring the Stories of Illness*. 1st ed. Oxford: Oxford University Press.

Claisse-Dauchy, Renée. 2000. *Médecine traditionnelle du Maghreb: rituels d'envoûtement et de guérison au Maroc*. French edition. Paris: L'Harmattan.

de Almeida-Filho, Naomar. 2006. "Modèles de la santé et de la maladie: remarques préliminaires pour une théorie générale de la santé." *Ruptures* 11, no. 1: 122–146.

de Pury, Sybille. 2005. *Comment on dit dans ta langue? Pratiques ethnopsychiatriques.* Divers Sciences Humaines. French edition. Empêcheurs de Penser en Rond. Paris: Le Seuil.

Dekens, Sandrine. 2007. Logiques sorcières: quand les accusations s'emballent. Accessed February 17, 2020, at http://osibouake.org /?Logiques-sorcieres-quand-les.

Devereux, George. 1970. *Essais d'ethnopsychiatrie generale.* Paris: Gallimard.

———. 1972. *Ethnopsychanalyse complémentariste.* Paris: Flammarion.

di Mbumba, Côme Khonde Ngoma. 2005. *Boma 1ère capitale de l'Etat Indépendant du Congo: 1885–1908. Espace Kinshasa.* French edition. Paris: L'Harmattan.

Evans-Pritchard, Edward E. 1972. *Sorcellerie, oracles et magie chez les Azandé.* Bibliothèque des sciences humaines. Paris: Gallimard.

Foucault, Michel, Daniel Defert, and François Ewald. 1994. *Dits et ecrits, 1954–1988, tome III: 1976–1979.* Bibliothèque des sciences humaines. Paris: Gallimard.

———. 2019. *Power: The Essential Works of Michel Foucault 1954–1984.* Vol. 3. Edited by James D. Faubion. Translated by Robert Hurley and others. Harmondsworth, UK: Penguin.

Good, Byron. 1994. *Medicine, Rationality, and Experience: An Anthropological Perspective.* Lewis Henry Morgan Lectures. 1st ed. Cambridge: Cambridge University Press.

Grenier, Bernard. 2004. "Décision médicale." In *Dictionnaire de la pensée médicale,* edited by Dominique Lecourt, 308–310. Paris: Presses Universitaires de France (PUF).

Guillaume-Hofnung, Michèle. 2001. *Hôpital et médiation.* French edition. Paris: L'Harmattan.

Hsieh, Elaine. 2016. *Bilingual Health Communication: Working with Interpreters in Cross-Cultural Care.* New York: Routledge.

Kirmayer, Laurence J., Danielle Groleau, Jaswant Guzder, Caminee Blake, and Eric Jarvis. 2003. "Cultural Consultation: A Model of Mental

Health Service for Multicultural Societies." *Canadian Journal of Psychiatry* 48: 145–153.

Kirmayer, Laurence J., Kenneth Fung, Cécile Rousseau, Hung Tat Lo, Peter Menzies, Jaswant Guzder, Soma Ganesan, Lisa Andermann, and Kwame McKenzie. 2012. "Guidelines for Training in Cultural Psychiatry." *Canadian Journal of Psychiatry* 57, no. 3, suppl.: 1–16.

Kirmayer, Laurence J., Jaswant Guzder, and Cécile Rousseau, eds. 2014. *International and Cultural Psychology. Cultural Consultation: Encountering the Other in Mental Health Care.* Berlin: Springer.

Kleinman, Arthur. 1981. *Patients and Healers in the Context of Culture: An Exploration of the Borderland Between Anthropology, Medicine, and Psychiatry.* Amsterdam: Amsterdam University Press.

Kline, A. S., trans. 2004. "Homer (c. 750 B.C.)—The Odyssey: Book I." Accessed November 28, 2019 at https://www.poetryintranslation.com/PITBR/Greek/Odyssey1.php.

Lachal, Jonathan, Mélanie Escaich, Serge Bouznah, Clémence Rousselle, Pascale De Lonlay, Pierre Canoui, Marie-Rose Moro, and Isabelle Durand-Zaleski. 2019. "Transcultural Mediation Programme in a Paediatric Hospital in France: Qualitative and Quantitative Study of Participants' Experience and Impact on Hospital Costs." *BMJ Open* 9, no. 11: e032498. Erratum in: *BMJ Open* 4 (April 26, 2020): e032498corr1.

Lagrange, Hughes. 2010. *Le Déni des cultures.* French edition. Paris: Le Seuil.

Laplante, Isabelle. 2009. Introduction—Pratiques Narratives. Accessed February 17, 2020, at http://www.pratiquesnarratives.com/-Introduction.html.

Laplanche, Jean, and Jean-Bertrand Pontalis. 2007. *Vocabulaire de la psychanalyse.* Dictionnaires Quadrige. French edition. Quadrige Dicos poche. Paris: Presses Universitaires de France (PUF).

Le Bossé, Yvan, and M. Lavallée. 1993. "Empowerment et psychologie communautaire: aperçu historique et perspective d'avenir." *Les Cahiers Internationaux De Psychologie Sociale* 18, no. 1: 7–20.

Le Breton, David. 1995. *Anthropologie de la douleur.* Collection Traversées. French edition. Paris: Éditions Métailié.

Lévy, Jacques, Emmanuelle Tricoire, and Quentin Skinner. 2007. "Concepts Only Have Histories." Accessed November 23, 2007, at https://www.espacestemps.net/articles/quentin-skinner/.

Mardus, Joseph-Charles. 1980. *Les Mille et une nuits, tome 2.* Paris: Robert Laffont.

Monseau, Grégoire. 2009. "Le récit-maladie, de l'expression du mal à l'éthique." *Transfaire et Cultures: Revue d'Anthropologie Médicale Clinique*, no. 1: 52–66.

Moro, Marie-Rose. 2011. *Psychothérapie transculturelle de l'enfant et de l'adolescent.* Psychothérapies. French edition. Paris: Dunod.

Napier, David, Michael Depledge, Michael Knipper, and Rebecca Lovell. 2017. *Culture Matters: Using a Cultural Context of Health Approach to Enhance Policy-Making.* Accessed January 20, 2020 at http://hdl.handle.net/10871/31607.

Nathan, Tobie. 1985. "L'enfant ancêtre." *Nouvelle Revue d'Ethnopsychiatrie*, no. 4: 7–8.

Nathan, Tobie. "Georges Devereux and Clinical Ethnopsychiatry." Translated by Catherine Grandsard. Accessed February 20, 2020 at https://www.ethnopsychiatrie.net/GDengl.htm.

———. 2013. *La Nouvelle Interprétation des rêves.* Odile Jacob, Poche Psycho. French edition. Paris: Odile Jacob.

Nathan, Tobie, and Catherine Lewertowski. 1998. *Le virus et le fétiche.* French edition. Paris: Odile Jacob.

Pergert, Pernilla, Solvig Ekblad, Karin Enskär, and Olle Björk. 2007. "Obstacles to Transcultural Caring Relationships: Experiences of Health Care Staff in Pediatric Oncology." *Journal of Pediatric Oncology Nursing* 24, no. 6: 314–328.

Ricoeur, Paul. 2005. "Devenir capable, être reconnu." *Esprit*, no. 7: 125–129. Translation accessed April 20, 2022 at https://plato.standord.edu/entries/ricoeur.

Rogers, Carl. 2018. *Le développement de la personne.* 2nd ed. Soins et Psy. French edition. Paris: Interéditions.

Sandron, Fréderic. 2011. "Transmission intergénérationnelle des normes et des valeurs: le famadihana dans les Hautes Terres malgaches." *Recherches familiales* 8, no. 1: 31–47.

Sluzki, Carlos. 2016. *The Presence of the Absent: Therapy with Families and Their Ghosts*. New York: Routledge.

Stengers, Isabelle, and Tobie Nathan. 2012. *Médecins et sorciers*. Expanded edition. Les Empêcheurs de penser en rond. French edition. Paris: La Découverte.

Taïeb, Olivier, Felicia Heidenreich, Thierry Baubet, and Marie-Rose Moro. 2005. "Donner un sens à la maladie: de l'anthropologie médicale à l'épidémiologie culturelle." *Médecine et Maladies Infectieuses* 35, no. 4: 173–185.

Thom, René. 1984. *Stabilité structurelle et morphogénèse: essai d'une théorie générale des modèles*. Paris: InterEditions.

Valéry, Paul. 1965. *Idée Fixe: A Duologue by the Sea*. Translated by David Paul in Paul Valéry, *Collected Works of Paul Valéry*, Vol. 5. New York: Bollingen Foundation.

Verrept, Hans. 2008. "Intercultural Mediation: An Answer to Health Care Disparities." In *Crossing Borders in Community Interpreting*, edited by Carmen Valero-Garcés and Anne Martin, 187–201. Amsterdam: John Benjamins Publishing.

Vuillard, Éric. 2021. *The War of the Poor*. Translated by Mark Polizotti. London: Pan Macmillan.

Vust, Delphine. 2010. "Psychodermatologie et moi-peau." *Psychothérapies* 30, no. 2: 65.

White, Michael, and David Epston. 2009. *Les moyens narratifs au service de la thérapie*. Brussels: Satas.

Yalom, Irvin. 2011. *When Nietzsche Wept: A Novel of Obsession*. Reprint. New York: Harper Perennial Modern Classics.

Zempléni, Andreas. 1985. "L'enfant Nit Ku Bon: un tableau psycho-pathologique traditionnel chez les Wolof et les Lebou du Sénégal." *Nouvelle revue d'ethnopsychiatrie*, no. 4: 9–41.

Index

Christianity, 25, 56, 57, 105, 132

chronic disease, 76, 139; allergy issues, 133; asthma, 126; atopic eczema, 126; chronic eczema, 124; chronic pain, 15; chronic painful pathology, 15; diabetic neuropathy, 65; post-traumatic stress disorder, 81; Pott's disease, 100, 103

codes, 16, 23; cultural, 16; of sociability, 142; of society, 16

complementarism, 14

complementarist method, 14

complementarity, 121, 140

comprehensive approach, 139

computers, 72

conflict, 17, 31, 32, 44, 66, 86, 89, 116, 117, 121, 130, 142; of allegiance, 118; current wives, 92; family, 23; France and Tunisia, 1, 147; military, 147; two brothers, 85, 87

crime, 108

cultural codes, 16

cultural difference, 8

cultural distance, 9

cultural intermingling, 8

cultural issues, 9

culturalist position, 9

culture, 3, 6, 9, 11, 13, 14, 31, 40, 54, 76, 85, 104, 107, 155; Jewish, 133

curse, 97–112, 135; family, 103, 107

customs, 45, 46, 105, 106, 117; Malagasy, 105

Dakar, 114, 115, 117, 118, 122

dead, 99; anima of, 106; body, 4; body of, 104; consulting, 106; cult of, 148; person, 104; raising, 56; sacred rites due to, 8; souls of, 106; therapeutic, 13; ties with, 11; to honor, 133; world of, 57

dead end, 13, 15, 89

Democratic Republic of Congo, 21, 24, 26, 28, 51, 149

depression, 42, 68, 73

depressive syndrome, 101

dermatologist, 49–53, 57, 60, 92, 124–128, 134, 138

dermatology, 124, 152; department, 49, 52; service, 60; unit, 124

Devereux, Georges, 14, 148

diabetes, 65, 66, 67, 70, 143, 150

diabetic neuropathy. *See* chronic disease

diagnosis, 10, 22; hypotheses of, 23; rare genetic disease, 51; spinal fibrosis, 37, 150

disease(s), 7–19, 36, 37, 39, 47, 53, 74, 99, 117–133, 136, 147–152; children's disease, 51; chronic, 76, 139; congenital, 150; course of, 4; dermatological, 51; expert in, 16; genetic, 50, 51, 52, 53, 56, 149; mechanisms of, 103; narrative of, 10; pair disease/illness, 10; pancreatic, 149; Pott's disease, 100, 103; skin, 128, 135; theories of, 11; tropical, 103

disorder(s), 13, 18, 58, 67; cause of, 41, 45; conception of, 41; definition of, 14; discourse on, 17; meaning of, 14; post-traumatic stress, 81; theories of, 67; treatment of, 148

doctors, 3, 11, 12, 16, 19, 24, 37, 47, 51, 54, 55, 94, 99, 104, 140; doctors' intervention, 40

dowries, 26

dreams, 68, 71, 101, 102, 120; nighttime, 69

eczema, 123–138

empathy, 119

empowerment, 157

ethical, 15

ethical approach, 113

ethical point of view, 140

ethnic group, 25, 36, 51, 140, 149, 152; Antakarana, 151; Azande, 26, 156; Bakongo, 25, 28, 57, 59, 61, 149, 150; Fulani, 80, 115, 116, 120, 149, 152; Jola, 152; Kabyle, 7; Khassonke, 36, 41, 43, 44, 46, 47, 48, 149; Kingwana, 25;

Lebu, 117, 150; Mandé, 79; Merina, 101, 151; Peuls, 80, 152; Sakalava, 151; Sarakhole, 149; Soninke, 36, 149; Susu, 79, 83, 84, 85, 87, 88, 89, 95; Swahili, 25, 149; Tsimihety, 151; Wolof, 119, 150, 159

ethnopsychiatry, 13, 14, 148, 156

etiological theories, 11; *ain*, 67, 74; evil eye, 3, 67, 144; evil spirits, 83, 84; Nit Ku Bon child-ancestor, 150; *shour*, 62, 65, 66, 70, 73, 74, 76

evangelical church, 53, 56

evil eye. *See* etiological theories

evil spirits, 83, 84. *See also* etiological theories

expert, 9, 134, 141; biomedical, 14; in disease, 16; position of, 40

expertise, 12, 13, 18, 145, 148

explanatory models, 11

family: anger, 33; arrangement, 58; belief system, 25; conflict(s), 23, 60, 110; curse, 103, 107; foster, 100, 102, 112; head of the, 47, 48, 74, 85, 87; history, 52, 101, 105, 111, 129; maternal, 28, 30; matters, 108, 109; members, 55, 95, 99, 146; name, 107, 130, 131; narrative, 47; network, 45; paternal, 28, 73, 111, 120, 133; protection, 70, 73, 130

fantasies, 128

folk medicine, 5

forefathers, 106

fortune teller, 66

fquih. *See* traditional healer

Fulani. *See* ethnic group

funeral rites, 55, 151; *famadihana*, 106, 110, 158

genetics: clues, 126; disease, 50–53, 56, 149; inheritance, 51; mutation, 55; predisposition, 67

gift(s), 69, 74; gift-giving, 59, 60; healing, 74

God, 79, 113, 119, 169; anger with, 205; faith in, 205; influence of, 39; water, 66; worship of a single, 98

Good, Byron, 11, 13

grandchildren, 28, 48, 71, 109

grandfather, 20, 28, 29, 31, 32, 72, 127, 131, 132, 133, 134, 137; maternal, 134; paternal, 2, 27, 126, 135

graves, 73, 105, 136; his grandparents' graves, 138; of grandparents, 145

Guinea, 79, 80, 91, 94, 96, 115, 116

Guinea-Bissau, 152

head of family, 47, 48, 74, 85, 87

healer, 66, 94, 116, 118, 119; traditional, 27, 44, 58; local, 55; initiated, 55; Muslim, 150

healthcare providers, 8, 12, 13, 15–18, 139, 140, 144–146, 153, 161

health system, 140

heart failure, 2

hell, 67, 103, 125

Hippocrates, 12

HIV, 10, 114, 147, 152

Holocaust, 133, 134, 153

Holy Land, 136

homosexual, 129

Hôpital Necker, 16, 20, 21, 49, 113, 114, 148

hospital practitioner, 16, 34, 62, 125

human beings, 54, 141

hysterical, 99

identities, 8

identity, 123, 133, 135, 141, 144; cultural, 123; Jewish, 133; specific identity, 190; transmission of, 133

illness, 9, 10, 13, 14, 15, 46, 47, 48, 58, 59, 67, 75, 103, 143, 145, 148; appearance of, 38; of a child, 58; discourse on, 14; Djibril's, 45; event, 18; experience of, 140; interpretations of, 10, 45, 144; meaning of, 11, 121; object, 4, 144; origin of, 45; patient's, 47; somatic, 73; story of, 143, 155; vision of, 8

mystical delirium, 109
mythical beings, 45

narrative, 5, 10, 18, 19, 40, 44, 45, 47, 64, 86, 103, 107, 114–119, 121, 130, 136, 142, 145; based medicine, 13; conversation, 143; family, 47; individual, 11; knowledge, 143; medical, 5, 40, 66, 115; medicine, 143, 155; of disease, 8; of the patient, 10; therapy, 143; thread, 10; worlds, 143
Nathan, Tobie, 10, 14–15, 26–27, 57, 141, 151
native language, 8, 15, 16, 47, 79, 140
ndepp, 117
ndoki, 26, 27, 31, 58
nefs, 68
nervous system, 40, 128, 150
neurological pain, 80
nganga, 26, 31, 55–58
nightmare(s), 66, 81, 83, 88, 90, 125, 151
Nit Ku Bon child, 150, 159

organ donation, 104, 105, 110
osteoarthritis, 64

painful pathology, 15
pain management, 15
pains, 22, 33, 64, 65, 76, 98, 110
paralysis, 99–101
paternal, 4, 57; grandfather, 2, 27, 72, 126, 135; grandmother, 116; relative(s), 23, 30; family, 28, 73, 111, 120, 133; uncle, 4, 24, 29; lineage(s), 57, 70, 74, 77, 111, 116, 133; clan, 29, 85
patrilineal, 25, 70, 74, 85, 116, 120, 133
Peuls. *See* Fulani
physiatrons, 4
physician(s), 4, 7, 9, 23, 67, 76, 98; hospital, 49, 50, 64, 67, 97, 115, 121
pilgrimage(s), 73, 74
polygamy, 91
possession, 57, 117
post-traumatic stress disorder. *See* chronic disease

Pott's disease. *See* chronic disease
power(s), 26, 73, 74, 84, 88, 156; healing, 73; of the invisible, 31; of narration, 143; of persuasion, 118, 125; unbelievable powers, 72
pregnancy, 51–53, 56, 61, 98, 99
pregnant, 51–53, 56, 61, 98, 100, 115
protection, 27, 44, 61, 70, 73, 74, 110, 120, 130, 133, 136; absence of, 117, 127; actions of, 145; family, 70, 73, 130; forms of, 46, 59, 74, 87; fundamental, 74; means of, 31, 47, 145
psychiatrist, 22, 25, 66, 109, 146, 151; department, 101; pediatric, 22
psychoanalysis, 3, 14, 128, 134
psychoanalyst, 83, 133
psychodermatologist, 128
psychodermatology, 124
psychosomatic, 124, 127, 128
psychotherapist, 14, 32, 129
psychotherapy, 14, 81, 126
purification, 61

rabbis, 133
rav, 135, 136, 147
religion(s), 25, 56, 132, 153
Republic of Zaïre, 51
resources, 18, 19, 94; of biomedical technical facilities, 16; community, 40, 146; of patients, 18
ritual(s), 4, 46, 56, 57, 75, 106, 147; Bakongo, 61; ceremonies, 117; funeral, 61; mortuary, 106; of possession, 117; protective, 75; of reconciliation, 96
rivalry, 44, 88, 92
Rogers, Carl, 119, 152, 158
rūḥ, 68

sacred children, 57
sacred texts, 135
sadaka, 74
Sakalava. *See* ethnic group
Sarakhole. *See* ethnic group
Satan, 134, 135
Scheherazade, 143

About the Authors

SERGE BOUZNAH was born on May 16, 1955, in Tunis. He is a public health physician specializing in transcultural clinical practice. In 1988, he founded one of the first services of transcultural mediation in France. At the Université Paris Descartes, he heads the department for mediation practice in transcultural situations, which leads to a specialized graduate diploma for physicians and other healthcare providers, as well as psychiatrists, psychologists, social workers, and other professionals. Dr. Bouznah has been the director of the Centre Babel at the Hôpital Cochin-Paris since December 2011.

CATHERINE LEWERTOWSKI is a physician who specializes in transcultural approaches. She currently oversees the primary health centers for mothers and children in the department of Seine Saint-Denis. Dr. Lewertowski is the author of *Soigner: Le virus et le fétiche* [Cure: The virus and the fetish] with Tobie Nathan, *Les enfants de Moissac, 1939–1945* [The children of Moissac, 1939–1945], and *Papi Nougat n'est pas mort* [Papi Nougat is not dead].

About the Translator

CARMELLA ABRAMOWITZ MOREAU studied social anthropology and English literature at the University of the Witwatersrand, Johannesburg. She holds a graduate certificate in teaching English as a second language from McGill University and an MA in translation from the University of London. She lives and works in Paris.

Printed in the United States
by Baker & Taylor Publisher Services